LISTEN TO THE MOCKINGBIRD

GREEN INTEGER BOOKS
Edited by Per Bregne
København/Los Angeles

Distributed in the United States by
Consortium Book Sales and Distribution
1045 Westgate Drive, Suite 90,
Saint Paul, Minnesota 55114-1065
Distributed in England and throughout Europe by
Turnaround Publisher Services
Unit 3, Olympia Trading Estate
Coburg Road, Wood Green, London N22 6TZ
44 (0)20 88293009

(323) 857-1115 / http://www.greeninteger.com

First Green Integer Edition 2005
Selection and Notes copyright ©2005 by Douglas Messerli
Introduction copyright ©2005 by Douglas Messerli
Back cover copy copyright ©2005 by Green Integer
All rights reserved.

Design: Per Bregne
Typography & Cover: Trudy Fisher
Cover Photographs (clockwise from left):
Stephen Foster Collins, Septimus Winner, Charles K. Harris,
and George F. Root

LIBRARY OF CONGRESS CATALOGING IN PUBLICATION DATA
Douglas Messerli, editor [1947]
*Listen to the Mockingbird: American Folksongs
and Popular Music Lyrics of the 19th Century*
ISBN: 1-892295-20-2
p. cm — Green Integer 130
I. Title II. Series

Green Integer books are published for Douglas Messerli
Printed in the United States of America on acid-free paper.

Listen to the Mockingbird

American Folksongs
and Popular Music Lyrics of the 19th Century

EDITED, WITH AN INTRODUCTION
BY DOUGLAS MESSERLI

GREEN INTEGER
KØBENHAVN & LOS ANGELES
2005

TABLE OF CONTENTS

Introduction

Folksongs (anonymous and traditional)

Popular Music

Listen to the Mockingbird

This book grew out of a short piece I was writing in 2003 about John Ford's movie *The Searchers*, in which the song "Shall We Gather at the River" is sung twice, if I remember correctly: once at a burial and once at a wedding. I was intrigued by the use of that song in the picture, and sought, on the internet, the complete lyrics. When I found those lyrics and music, I decided briefly to look at other songs of the period, and suddenly I found myself assembling a short anthology of 19th century popular music lyrics.

Certainly this had been done before. Dover Press, for example, long had a book of lyrics and music of 19th century songs in print; and there have been others. But I felt that a new edition, with new selections and a fresh outlook, would be useful. Coincidently, soon after I had begun research I traveled to Frankfurt for the annual Frankfurt Bookfair, and there had dinner with several Scandinavian (Norwegian, Swedish,

Danish, and Icelandic) editors, publishers and agents. After an excellent dinner in one of my favorite Frankfurt restaurants, the group began singing folksongs from their different languages. Almost all knew the songs, and joined in. One or two individuals knew all the lyrics of the several stanzas of each piece they sang, reminding the others, the fact of which greatly surprised me. Certainly I knew the importance of songs to these cultures; when I was sixteen I had attended a Norwegian folk high school, where each day we carried a book of the lyrics of national hymns and popular folksongs to classes; as we stood for the arriving teachers, he or she called out a number, and we turned to that particular song in the little book and sang it before getting down to work. But I was still amazed — and delighted — to see how this group of intellectuals had continued in their love of this singing tradition. When they asked me to sing an American song, I could remember no lyrics, and I was forced to perform "Coming 'Round the Mountain" with my own lyrics, made up on the spot. As one of them asked, "You don't have this tradition in America?" No, we had not, I responded, but I promised by the next year I would have published a book which would serve me. In short, that incident encouraged me to move more quickly with my research.

I am not so certain now that the book is completed, however, that I wish to share it with those Scandinavian friends. Certainly there are lovely folksongs and spirituals that would nicely represent America. Most of the African-American spirituals, "All God's Chillun Got Wings," "Ezekiel's Wheel," "Go Down Moses," and "Nobody Knows the Trouble I've Seen" among them, are truly wondrous songs, simple and yet meaningful. And other songs of faith, among them "Bringing in the Sheaves," "Shall We Gather at the River" and my favorite, the Shaker hymn "Simple Gifts," are beautiful representations of 19th century American expression and belief. A few of the chanteys and folksongs, "The Drunken Sailor," "Shenandoah," and "Bought Me a Cat," are also quite fun to perform and have charming lyrics. But most of the others included in this collection of 78 songs, at the very least, are strange, and a great number are bizarre and quite perverse. Take, for example, the popular

"Clementine," a song of which most of us know the chorus and perhaps a few lyrics. You may recall that it is about a miner, his daughter Clementine, and her death. When one reads the complete lyrics, he quickly realizes that this song is a comic number that takes the listener into the rather frightening world of a miner, who because he could not swim, allowed his daughter to drown; his sorrow is based, quite clearly, on his deep love for her — which it is suggested went beyond the usual familial relationship. The young girl, we are told, named after her dead mother, is the miner's "favorite nugget," over whom he "frets and pines" until he recalls that he has another, similarly beautiful daughter at home, whom when he kisses, makes him utterly forget Clementine. The little missing dog in "Der Deitcher's Dog" may have been ground up as sausage. "Grandfather's Clock" is a song about an anthropomorphized clock that rings out a long-dead alarm at the death of its owner and itself stops dead. The theater song "Reuben and Rachel" is a duet in which a representative of each sex imagines how pleasant the world would be without the other. "The Little Brown Jug" is a song about an alcoholic husband and wife — one a lover of gin, the other of rum — who celebrate the fact they have nothing save each other and their jugs. The standard classic "After the Ball" recounts the story of an unmarried man, who because he saw his fiancée in the arms of another man, cast her out of his life; but the other man, he ultimately discovers, was only her brother. The Buffalo Gal of the famous song is quite beautiful, perhaps, but has feet that take up the whole sidewalk and make it very difficult for the narrator to dance with her under the light of the moon. Even the beloved "Jingle Bells" is about a couple who, crashing into a snow bank, are laughed at and dismissed by other passing sleighers. And those are among the songs in this volume that are most innocent.

A great part of 19th century music and lyrics was devoted, quite understandably, to the Civil War. And these songs represent the battle between members of the same country in an often painfully comic way. Julia Ward Howe's great "Battle Hymn of the Republic" was adapted from Patrick S. Gilmore's gory "John Brown's Body," which begins with the stanza "John Brown's

Body lies a-moulderin' in the grave," and gradually shifts to the prediction that "They will hang Jeff Davis to a sour apple tree," punctuated, of course, with the famed chorus of "Glory! Glory! Hallelujah!" Walter Kittredge's renowned "Tenting Tonight on the Old Camp Ground" begins with good cheer and friends, but soon shifts to the dead and dying on the same camp ground. Ethel Beers' "All Quiet Along the Potomac" is a true masterwork of black humor, as she observes "All quiet along the Potomac, tonight, / Except here and there a stray picket / Is shot as he walks on his beat to and fro." A private or two will not count in the news as long as there is "Not an officer lost." "The darkeys" shout, the turkeys gobble, and the "sweet potatoes" start from the ground as the Union troops march through Georgia in "Marching Through Georgia." The rousing marching song, "Tramp! Tramp! Tramp!" is sung from a prison cell in what is evidently the Andersonville camp, where over 13,000 men died. And perhaps the most silly of all Civil War songs is "Jeff in Petticoats," whose lyrics recount a version of a true story about Jefferson Davis, who, when he was arrested by the Union troops, was found dressed in his wife's overcoat. The lyrics were written by the young man, George Cooper, with whom the greatest American composer of the century, Stephen Collins Foster, composed his last songs, and who ultimately was the one who discovered Foster drunk and dying. Americans clearly will find little of which to be proud in their songs of the Civil War.

The most troubling aspect of the lyrics of the 19th century are the racial and national stereotypes they represent. The great majority of the popular songs of the century were written for the minstrel shows, and famed works such as "Turkey in the Straw," known at the time as "Zip Coon," "Jim Crack Corn," "Susanna," "De Camptown Races," "Swanee River," "My Old Kentucky Home," "Dixie," "Old Black Joe," and "Kingdom Coming," were written for minstrel groups such as the Virginia, Buckley, and Christy Minstrels; and, although today they are often "cleaned up" for popular consumption, they were originally written in Black dialect, relying on stock humor and clichés that the whites had established about Blacks. The "Zip Coon," the Black urban dandy, and "Jim Crow," the guileless plantation slave, were at the heart of the vast majority of 19th century popular music lyrics, and their presentation of these and other figures, despite their often humorous intentions, were based on ignorance, prejudice, and hate.

The only positive thing that one can say about these popular songs is that they help us to perceive that throughout the century the most joyful and humorous music — music to which one danced and which expressed everyday pleasures — was perceived in the white imagination as having something to do with African Americans. And after the Civil War, when Blacks could begin to perform in minstrel shows themselves, several of the most talented minstrel composers — writers such as Sam Lucas (composer of "Ring Dem Heavenly Bells" and "My Thoughts Are of Thee") and James Allen Bland (composer of "Carry Me Back to Old Virginny," and "Oh, Dem Golden Slippers" along with many other popular works) — were African Americans, who, while still using dialect, shifted the presentation of people of their race from mere stock types to actual human beings of more complex thinking and emotions. These composers reveal the direct influence of the early African-American spirituals, and link the whole of the 19th century musical tradition to ragtime and, ultimately, to jazz.

As the minstrel shows began to die out, moreover, the popular songs at the end of the century — works like "The Sidewalks of New York" and "The Band Played On" — performed in vaudeville, shifted their subjects to love and focused more on an expression of community sentiment. The sense of isolation and estrangement so commonly expressed throughout the century was gradually transformed to lyrics representing public activity, dancing in social clubs, bicycling through the city, and "tripping the light fantastic" down the city "sidewalks."

In short, just as the culture at large shifted from the perspective of a people living in rural settings still in the wilderness to a more and more urbane and cosmopolitan consciousness, so too did the lyrics and music shift from an expression of what might be described as almost a xenophobic paranoia — a terror of other cultures and races — to a vision of a more communal sensibility that we find in the hundreds of theatrical lyrics of the early part of the 20th century. Yet, despite this, even today we might still recognize some of those dark elements of the American culture represented in these early lyrics. There remains always somewhere in American music the sound of a mockingbird, something that attempts to mock us through imitation, but is not quite the same as "us" — whoever we believe ourselves to be — and reminds us of our frailties and all that we have lost and may yet lose. As Ira Gershwin expressed it in his 1937 song from the film *Shall We Dance*, since you say "either" and I "either," you say "neither" and I say "neither," we may have to call the whole thing off.

— Douglas Messerli

ALL GOD'S CHILLUN GOT WINGS

traditional African-American spiritual

I got a robe, you got a robe
All o' God's chillun got a robe
When I get to heab'n I'm goin' to put on my
    robe
I'm goin' to shout all ovah God's Heab'n,
Heab'n, Heab'n
Ev'rybody talkin' 'bout heab'n ain't goin'
    dere
Heab'n, Heab'n
I'm goin' to shout all ovah God's Heab'n

I got a wings, you got a wings
All o' God's chillun got a wings
When I get to heab'n I'm goin' to put on my
    wings
I'm goin' to fly all ovah God's Heab'n
Heab'n, Heab'n
Ev'rybody talkin' 'bout heab'n ain't goin'
    dere
Heab'n, Heab'n
I'm goin' to fly all ovah God's Heab'n

I got a harp, you got a harp
All o' God's chillun got a harp
When I get to heab'n I'm goin' to take up my
 harp
I'm goin' to play all ovah God's Heab'n
Heab'n, Heab'n
Ev'rybody talkin' 'bout heab'n ain't goin'
 dere
Heab'n, Heab'n
I'm goin' to play all ovah God's Heab'n

I got shoes, you got shoes
All o' God's chillun got shoes
When I get to heab'n I'm goin' to put on my
 shoes
I'm goin' to walk all ovah God's Heab'n
Heab'n, Heab'n
Ev'rybody talkin' 'bout heab'n ain't goin'
 dere
Heab'n, Heab'n
I'm goin' to walk all ovah God's Heab'n

Bought Me a Cat

traditional song

Bought me a cat and the cat pleased me,
I fed my cat under yonder tree.
Cat goes fiddle-i-fee.

Bought me a hen and the hen pleased me,
I fed my hen under yonder tree.
Hen goes chimmy-chuck, chimmy-chuck,
Cat goes fiddle-i-fee.

Bought me a duck and the duck pleased me,
I fed my duck under yonder tree.
Duck goes quack, quack,
Hen goes chimmy-chuck, chimmy-chuck,
Cat goes fiddle-i-fee.

Bought me a goose and the goose pleased me
I fed my goose under yonder tree.
Goose goes hissy, hissy,
Duck goes quack, quack,
Hen goes chimmy-chuck, chimmy-chuck,
Cat goes fiddle-i-fee.

Bought me a sheep and the sheep pleased
    me,
I fed my sheep under yonder tree.
Sheep goes baa, baa,
Goose goes hissy, hissy,
Duck goes quack, quack,
Hen goes chimmy-chuck, chimmy-chuck,
Cat goes fiddle-i-fee.

Bought me a pig and the pig pleased me,
I fed my pig under yonder tree.
Pig goes oink, oink,
Sheep goes baa, baa,
Goose goes hissy, hissy,
Duck goes quack, quack,
Hen goes chimmy-chuck, chimmy-chuck,
Cat goes fiddle-i-fee.

Bought me a cow and the cow pleased me,
I fed my cow under yonder tree.
Cow goes moo, moo,
Pig goes oink, oink,
Sheep goes baa, baa,
Goose goes hissy, hissy,
Duck goes quack, quack,

Hen goes chimmy-chuck, chimmy-chuck,
Cat goes fiddle-i-fee.

Bought me a horse and the horse pleased me,
I fed my horse under yonder tree.
Horse goes neigh, neigh,
Cow goes moo, moo,
Pig goes oink, oink,
Sheep goes baa, baa,
Goose goes hissy, hissy,
Duck goes quack, quack,
Hen goes chimmy-chuck, chimmy-chuck,
Cat goes fiddle-i-fee.

Bought me a dog and the dog pleased me,
I fed my dog under yonder tree.
Dog goes bow-wow, bow-wow,
Horse goes neigh, neigh,
Cow goes moo, moo,
Pig goes oink, oink,
Sheep goes baa, baa,
Goose goes hissy, hissy,
Duck goes quack, quack,
Hen goes chimmy-chuck, chimmy-chuck,
Cat goes fiddle-i-fee.

This traditional folk song, reintroduced in the 20th century by composer Aaron Copland, has, quite obviously, a lot in common with the standard "Old McDonald's Farm."

CARRY ME BACK TO GREEN PASTURES

traditional African-American song

Carry me back to green, green pastures,
Dat's where I long to be;
Carry me back to green pastures,
Dat am de place for me.
I want to see de fields of cotton,
Close to dat Swanee shore;
I want to hear my mammy callin',
Down by dat cabin door.
Ole rockin' chair jes' keeps on swingin',
Rockin' me to and fro;
Sometimes I hear de angels singin',
"Chariots a-swingin' low."
I know dat dare's a land of promise
Waitin' for weary souls,
Carry me back to green, green pastures
Down where de Jordan rolls.

The noted singer Paul Robeson made this song, "All God's Chillun Got Wings," and others famous in recordings of the early 1930s.

Coming 'Round the Mountain

traditional song, tune from the African-American spiritual "When the Chariot Comes"

She'll be coming 'round the mountain when
she comes
She'll be coming 'round the mountain when
she comes
She'll be coming 'round the mountain, she'll
be coming 'round the mountain,
She'll be coming 'round the mountain when
she comes.

She'll be driving six white horses when she
comes
etc.

Oh, we'll all come out to meet her when she
comes
etc.

We will kill the old red rooster when she
comes
etc.

We'll all have chicken 'n dumplin's when she
   comes

etc.

We'll all be shoutin' "Halleluja" when she
   comes

etc.

This popular American song has various alternative
verses.

The Drunken Sailor (What Shall We Do with a Drunken Sailor?)

traditional chantey

What'll we do with a drunken sailor,
What'll we do with a drunken sailor,
What'll we do with a drunken sailor,
Earl-aye in the morning?

> *Chorus:*
> Way hay and up she rises
> Patent blocks o' diff'rent sizes,
> Way hay and up she rises
> Earl-aye in the morning

Other lyrics (followed each by the chorus)
1) Sling him in the long boat till he's sober,
2) Keep him there and make 'im bale 'er,
3) Pull out the plug and wet him over,
4) Take 'im and shake 'im, try an' wake 'im,
5) Trice him up in a runnin' bowline,
6) Give 'im a taste of the bo'sun's rope-end,
7) Give 'im a dose of salt and water,
8) Stick on 'is back a mustard plaster,

9) Shave his belly with a rusty razor,
10) Send him up the crow's nest till he falls down,
11) Tie him to the taffrail when she's yardarm under,
12) Put him in the scuppers with a hose-pipe on him,
13) Soak 'im in oil till he sprouts flippers,
14) Put him in the guard room till he's sober,
15) Put him to bed with the captain's daughter,
16) Take the Baby and call it Bo'sun,
17) Turn him over and drive him windward,
18) Put him in the scuffs until the horse bites on him,
19) Heave him by the leg and with a rung console him,
20) That's what we'll do with the drunken sailor,

This song, known to be at least as old as 1841, is a windlass and capstan work song that is associated with Massachusetts. The "daughter" in stanza 15 is also something akin to the cat-o'-nine-tails.

Ezekiel's Wheel

traditional African-American spiritual

Ezekiel saw a wheel a-turning,
Way in the middle of the air,
A wheel within a wheel a-turning,
Way in the middle of the air,
And the little wheel turned by faith,
And the big wheel turned
By the grace of God,
Ezekiel saw a wheel a-turning,
Way in the middle of the air.

Ezekiel saw a flame a-burning,
Way in the middle of the air,
A flame within a flame a-burning,
Way in the middle of the air,
And the little flame burned by faith,
And the big flame burned
By the grace of God,
Ezekiel saw a flame a-burning,
Way in the middle of the air.

Go Down, Moses

traditional African-American spiritual

When Israel was in Egypt's land,
Let my people go!
Oppressed so hard they could not stand,
Let my people go!

> *Chorus:*
> Go down, Moses,
> Way down in Egypt's land.
> Tell old Pharaoh
> To let my people go!

"Thus spoke the Lord," bold Moses said
"Let my people go!
If not, I'll smite your firstborn dead.
Let my people go!"

> *Chorus*

No more shall they in bondage toil
Let my people go!

Let them come out of Egypt's spoil
Let my people go!

Chorus

The Lord told Moses what to do
Let my people go!
To lead the Hebrew children through
Let my people go!

Chorus

O come along Moses, you'll not get lost
Let my people go!
Stretch out your rod and come across
Let my people go!

Chorus

As Israel stood by the water side
Let my people go!
At God's command it did divide
Let my people go!

Chorus

When they reached the other shore
Let my people go!
They sang a song of triumph o'er
Let my people go!

Chorus

Pharaoh said he'd go across
Let my people go!
But Pharaoh and his host were lost
Let my people go!

Chorus

O let us all from bondage flee
Let my people go!
And let us all in Christ be free
Let my people go!

Chorus

You need not always weep and mourn
Let my people go!
And wear these slav'ry chains forlorn
Let my people go!

Chorus

Your foes shall not before you stand
Let my people go!
And you'll possess fair Canaan's land.
Let my people go!

Chorus

I've Been Working on the Railroad

traditional song

I've been working on the railroad
All the livelong day
I've been working on the railroad
Just to pass the time away

Can't you hear the whistle blowing
Rise up so early in the morn
Can't you hear the captain shouting
Dinah, blow your horn

Dinah, won't you blow
Dinah, won't you blow
Dinah, won't you blow your horn
Dinah, won't you blow
Dinah, won't you blow
Dinah, won't you blow your horn

Someone's in the kitchen with Dinah
Someone's in the kitchen I know
Someone's in the kitchen with Dinah
Strumming on the old banjo, and singing

Fie, fi, fiddly i o
Fie, fi, fiddly i o
Fie, fi, fiddly i o
Strumming on the old banjo

This song, of uncertain origin, has been traced by some to a Louisiana levee song of African-Americans. Others believe it to be adapted by the Irish work gangs in the West from an old hymn. The verses "Dinah" and "Someone's in the kitchen" appear to be later additions.

Joshua Fit de Battle ob Jericho

traditional African-American spiritual

Joshua fit de battle ob Jericho, Jericho, Jericho,
Joshua fit de battle ob Jericho
An de walls come tumblin' down.
You may talk about yo' king ob Gideon, you
    may
Talk about yo' man ob Saul, dere's none like
    good
Ol' Joshua, at de battle ob Jericho.
Up to de walls ob Jericho, He march'd wid
    spear in han'
"Go blow dem ram horns," Joshua cried
"Kase de battle am in my han."
Den de lam' ram sheep horns begin to blow
De trumpets begin to soun', Joshua
    commanded
De chillem to shout, an' de walls come
    tumblin' down
Dat mornin' Joshua fit de battle ob Jericho,
    Jericho, Jericho,
Joshua fit de battle ob Jericho,
An de walls come tumblin' down.

Nobody Knows the Trouble
I've Seen

traditional African-American spiritual

Oh, nobody knows the trouble I've seen,
Nobody knows but Jesus,
Nobody knows the trouble I've seen
Glory Hallelujah!

Sometimes I'm up, sometimes I'm down; Oh,
   yes, Lord;
Sometimes I'm almost to the ground; Oh,
   yes, Lord.
Although you see me going along; Oh, yes,
   Lord;
I have my trials here below; Oh, yes Lord;

[First stanza repeated]

The Old Chisholm Trail

traditional cowboy song

Come along boys and listen to my tale,
I'll tell you of my troubles on the old
  Chisholm trail.

Chorus:
  Come a ti yi yippee, come a ti yi yea.
  Come a ti yi yippee, come a ti yi yea.

Oh, a ten-dollar hoss and a forty-dollar
  saddle,
And I'm starting up the hill just punchin'
  Texas cattle.

Chorus

I wake in the mornin' afore daylight,
And afore I sleep the moon shines bright.

Chorus

It's cloudy in the west, a-lookin' like rain,

And my durned old slicker's in the wagon
   again.

Chorus

No chaps, no slicker, and it's pourin' down
   rain,
And I swear, by gosh, I'll never night-herd
   again.

Chorus

Feet in the stirrups and seat in the saddle,
I hung and rattled with them long-horn
   cattle.

Chorus

The wind commenced to blow, and the rain
   began to fall,
Hit looked, by grab, like we was goin' to lose
   'em all.

Chorus

I don't give a darn if they never do stop;
I'll ride as long as an eight-day clock.

Chorus

We rounded 'em up and put 'em on the cars,
And that was the last of the old Two Bars.

Chorus

Oh, it's bacon and beans most every day,
I'd as soon be a-eatin' prairie hay.

Chorus

I went to the boss to draw my roll,
He had it figgered out I was nine dollars in
   the hole.

Chorus

Goin' back to town to draw my money,
Goin' back home to see my honey.

Chorus

With my knees in the saddle and my seat in
the sky,
I'll quit punchin' cows in the sweet by and
by.

Chorus

This traditional cowboy song was made most famous,
perhaps, in the 20th century as a song sung often by
performer Gene Autry.

POLLY WOLLY DOODLE

traditional song

Oh I went down South for to see my Sal,
Singin' Polly Wolly Doodle all the day,
For my Sal she was a spunky gal.
Sing Polly Wolly Doodle all the day.

> *Chorus:*
> Fare thee well, fare thee well,
> Fare thee well my fairy Fay,
> For I'm off to Lou'siana for to see my Susy
>   Anna
> Singin' Polly Wolly Doodle all the day.

Oh my Sally was such a maiden fair,
Singin' Polly Wolly Doodle all the day,
With her curly eyes and her laughing hair.
Sing Polly Wolly Doodle all the day.

> *Chorus*

Oh I went to bed but it weren't no use
Singin' Polly Wolly Doodle all the day,

'Cause my feet stuck out for a chicken's
  roost.
Sing Polly Wolly Doodle all the day.

Chorus

From behind the barn, down upon my knees
Singin' Polly Wolly Doodle all the day,
I could swear I heard that ol' chicken
  sneeze.
Sing Polly Wolly Doodle all the day.

Chorus

Oh a grasshopper sat on a railroad track
Singin' Polly Wolly Doodle all the day,
Was a-pickin his teeth with a carpet tack.
Sing Polly Wolly Doodle all the day.

Chorus

An' he sneezed so hard with the 'hoopin'
  cough
Singin' Polly Wolly Doodle all the day,

That he sneezed his head an' his tail right off
Sing Polly Wolly Doodle all the day.

Chorus

RED RIVER VALLEY

traditional Canadian or American song

From this valley they say you are going
We will miss your bright eyes and sweet
 smile
For they say you are taking the sunshine
That has brightened our path for a while.

 Chorus:
 Come and sit by my side if you love me
 Do not hasten to bid me adieu
 But remember the Red River Valley
 And the cowboy who loved you so true.

Won't you think of the valley you're leaving
O how lonely, how sad it will be?
O think of the fond heart you're breaking
And the grief you are causing to me.

 Chorus

As you go to your home by the ocean
May you never forget those sweet hours
That we spent in the Red River Valley
And the love we exchanged mid the flowers.

Chorus

There is a great deal of controversy about this traditional song. Popularized in the 20th century by cowboy performers such as Gene Autry and Roy Rogers, many have presumed the song was of Texan origin. Others have argued that it was adapted from a song about the Mohawk Valley in upstate New York. Still others insist that the song originated among British troops who came to Manitoba and the Red River Valley there to put down the Metis rebellion of the late 1860s. There are, accordingly, many alternative lyrics.

ROLL JORDAN, ROLL

traditional African-American spiritual

Roll Jordan, roll
Roll Jordan, roll
I wanter go to heav'n when I die
To hear ol' Jordan roll
O brethren
Roll Jordan, roll
Roll Jordan, roll
I wanter go to heav'n when I die
To hear ol' Jordan roll

Oh, brothers you oughter been dere
Yes my Lord
A-sittin' in the Kingdom
To hear ol' Jordan roll
Sing it over
Oh, sinner you oughter been dere
Yes my Lord
A-sittin' in the Kingdom
To hear ol' Jordan roll.

SHENANDOAH

traditional chantey

Missouri, she's a mighty river
Way-aye, you rolling river
The redskin's camp lies on its borders,
A way — we're bound away
'cross the wide Missouri!

The white man loved the Indian maid,
Way-aye, you rolling river!
With notions his canoe was laden
A way — we're bound away
'cross the wide Missouri!

Oh Shenandoah, I love your daughter
Way-aye, you rolling river
I'll take her 'cross yon rolling water
A way — we're bound away
'cross the wide Missouri!

The Chief disdained the trader's dollars,
Way-aye, you rolling river
My daughter you shall never follow

A way — we're bound away
'cross the wide Missouri!

For seven years I courted Sally,
Way-aye, you rolling river
For seven more I longed to have her
A way — we're bound away
'cross the wide Missouri!

She said she would not be my lover
Way-aye, you rolling river
Because I was a tarry sailor
A way — we're bound away
'cross the wide Missouri!

At last there came a Yankee skipper
Way-aye, you rolling river
He winked his eye, and he tipped his flipper
A way — we're bound away
'cross the wide Missouri!

He sold the Chief that fire-water
Way-aye, you rolling river
And 'cross the river he stole his daughter

A way — we're bound away
'cross the wide Missouri!

Oh Shenandoah! I long to hear you,
Way-aye, you rolling river
Across that wide and rolling river
A way — we're bound away
'cross the wide Missouri!

Dating at least as far back as the 1820s, this chantey
song, used with the windlass, capstan, and winches
for loading cargo, is said to have originated among
the early American rivermen or Canadian voyageurs.
Some believe it was a land song before it was brought
to the sea. In any event, it was extremely popular on
both land and sea, having various names over the
years, including "Shennydore," "The Wide Missouri,"
"The Wild Mizzourye," "The World of Misery-Solid
Fas," "The Oceanida," and "Rolling River." Shenandoah was an Indian chief living on the Missouri River.

SHORT'NIN' BREAD

traditional African-American song

Put on de skillet, put on de lead,
Mammy's gonna make a little short'nin'
    bread.
Dat ain't all she's gonna do,
Mammy's gonna make a little coffee too.

Chorus:
    Mammy's little baby loves short'nin',
        short'nin',
    Mammy's little baby loves short'nin' bread.

Three little darkies lying in bed
Two was sick an' the other 'most dead.
Send for the doctor, the doctor said,
"Feed dose darkies on short'nin' bread!"

Chorus

Slip to de kitchen, slip up de lead,
Slip ma pockets full of short'nin' bread.

Stole de skillet, stole de lead,
Stole de gal to make short'nin' bread.

Chorus

Dey caught me wi' de skillet, dey caught me
  wi' de lead,
Caught me wi' de gal makin' short'nin'
  bread.
Six dollars fo' de skillet, paid six dollars fo'
  de lead,
Spent six months in jail eatin' short'nin'
  bread.

Chorus

Swing Low, Sweet Chariot

traditional African-American spiritual

Chorus:
Swing low, sweet chariot,
Coming for to carry me home.
Swing low, sweet chariot,
Coming for to carry me home.

I looked over Jordan and what did I see,
Coming for to carry me home!
A band of angels coming after me,
Coming for to carry me home.

Chorus

If you get there before I do,
Coming for to carry me home!
Tell all my friends I'se a-coming too,
Coming for to carry me home.

Chorus

AMERICA (1832)

lyrics by Rev. Samuel Francis Smith
music by Henry Cary, popular in England as
"God Save the King (Queen)"

My country, 'tis of thee,
Sweet land of liberty,
Of thee I sing;
Land where my fathers died
Land of the pilgrims' pride
From every mountain side
Let freedom ring.

My native country, thee,
Land of the noble free
Thy name I love;
I love thy rocks and rills
Thy woods and templed hills
My heart with rapture thrills
Like that above.

No more shall tyrants here
With haughty steps appear
And soldier bands

No more shall tyrants dread
Above the patriot dead
No more our blood be shed
By alien hands.

Let music swell the breeze
And ring from all the trees
Sweet freedom's song
Let all that breathes partake
Let mortal tongues awake
Let rocks their silence break
The sound prolong.

Our fathers' God to Thee
Author of liberty
To Thee we sing
Long may our land be bright
With freedom's holy light
Protect us by Thy might
Our God our King.

American minister and writer Samuel Francis Smith (1808-1895) was one of the editors of *The Psalmist*, one of the most influential of the American Baptist collections. Smith deleted the third verse of the above text, and, in the original, transposed the 5th and 6th line of the fourth verse.

The tune, now the British national anthem, was based on a German song "Thesarus Musicus" attributed to Henry Cary (1740).

Zip Coon (Turkey in the Straw)

(1834)

Anonymous

O ole Zip Coon he is a larned skoler,
O ole Zip Coon he is a larned skoler,
O ole Zip Coon he is a larned skoler,
Sings possum up a gum tree an coony in a
    holler,
Possum up a gum tree, coony on a stump,
Possum up a gum tree, coony on a stump,
Possum up a gum tree, coony on a stump,
Den over dubble trubble, Zip Coon will
    jump.

> *Chorus:*
> O Zip a duden duden duden zip a duden
>   day,
> O Zip a duden duden duden zip a duden
>   day,
> O Zip a duden duden duden zip a duden
>   day,
> Zip a duden duden duden zip a duden day.

O it's old Suky blue skin, she is in lub wid
    me,
I went the udder arter noon to take a dish ob
    tea;
What do you tink now, Suky hab for supper,
Why chicken foot an possum heel, widout
    any butter.

Chorus

Did you eber see the wild goose, sailing on
    de ocean,
O de wild goose motion is a bery pretty
    notion;
Ebry time de wild goose, beckons to de
    swaller,
You hear him google google google google
    goller.

Chorus

I went down to Sandy Hollar tother
    arternoon
And the first man I chanced to meet war ole
    Zip Coon;

Ole Zip Coon he is a natty scholar,
For he plays upon de Banjo "Cooney in de
  hollar."

  Chorus

My old Missus she's mad wid me,
Kase I wouldn't go wid her into Tennessee
Massa build him barn and put in de fodder
Twas dis ting and dat ting on ting or odder.

  Chorus

I pose you heard ob de battle New Orleans,
Whar ole Gineral Jackson gib de British
  beans;
Dare de Yankee boys ob de job so slick,
For dey cotch old Packenham an rowed him
  up de creek.

  Chorus

I hab many tings to tork about but just don't
  know wich come first,

So here de toast to ole Zip Coon before he
   gin to rust;
May he hab de pretty girls, like de King ob
   ole,
To sing dis song so many times, 'fore he turn
   to mole.

Chorus

When the Virginia Minstrels, headed by Daniel
Decatur Emmett, first began performing separate
minstrel productions, the two basic stereotypes of the
minstrel performers — "Zip Coon" (the urban dandy)
and "Jim Crow" (the guileless plantation slave) de-
veloped into two separate shows, each relying on
stock humor and clichés. "Zip Coon," with music from
"Turkey in the Straw," was performed by George
Washington Dixon, one of the great black imperson-
ators.

   This song, believed by some to be written by
Dixon, was his greatest hit. Others have suggested
the work was written by George Nichols or Bob
Farrell.

Rocked in the Cradle of the Deep

(1840)

lyrics by Emma Hart Willard
music by Joseph Philip Knight

Rocked in the cradle of the deep,
I lay me down in peace to sleep;
Secure I rest upon the wave,
For Thee, O Lord, hast power to save.
I know Thou wilt not slight my call,
For Thou dost mark the sparrow's fall:

> *Chorus:*
> And calm and peaceful is my sleep,
> Rocked in the cradle of the deep.
> [repeated]

And such the trust that still were mine,
Tho' stormy winds swept o'er the brine;
Or tho' the tempest's fiery breath
Rous'd me from sleep to wreck and death,
In ocean cave still safe with Thee,
The hope of immortality;

Chorus

Emma Willard wrote this song in 1832 on a journey across the Atlantic on her return from Europe. The lyrics were put to music by Joseph P. Knight, who for one year taught music at the school in Vermont that Mrs Willard ran. Knight returned to England as a clergyman in the parish of St Agnes in the Scilly Isle. He composed over 200 songs.

We Won't Go Home Till Morning
(1842)

lyricist and composer unknown

We're all met here together,
We're all met here together,
We're all met here together,
To eat and drink good cheer;
To eat and drink good cheer;
To eat and drink good cheer;

> *Chorus:*
> For we won't go home till morning,
> We won't go home till morning,
> We won't go home till morning,
> Till daylight does appear.

We'll sing, we'll dance and be merry,
We'll sing, we'll dance and be merry,
We'll sing, we'll dance and be merry,
And kiss the lasses dear;
And kiss the lasses dear;
And kiss the lasses dear;

Chorus

The girls we love them dearly,
The girls we love them dearly,
The girls we love them dearly,
And they love us, tis clear;
And they love us, tis clear;
And they love us, tis clear;

Chorus

Coda:
Away, away, away
Away, away, away,
For now we must be going,
For now we must be going,
For now we must be going,
Away, away, away.

The publisher of this popular song was Oliver Ditson of Boston.

Buffalo Gals (1844)

lyrics and music by Cool White

Refrain:
Buffalo Gals, won't you come out tonight,
Come out tonight, come out tonight.
Buffalo Gals, won't you come out tonight
And dance by the light of the moon.

As I was walking down the street,
Down the street, down the street,
A pretty little gal I chanced to meet,
Oh, she was fair to see.

Refrain

I stopped her and we had a talk,
Had a talk, had a talk,
Her feet took up the whole sidewalk
And left no room for me.

Refrain

I asked her if she'd have a dance,
Have a dance, have a dance,
I thought that I might have a chance
To shake a foot with her.

Refrain

I danced with a gal with a hole in her
   stockin',
And her heel kept a-knockin' and her toes
   kept a-rockin'
I danced with a gal with a hole in her
   stockin'
And we danced by the light of the moon.

Refrain

This famous American song was featured in Frank
Capra's *It's a Wonderful Life*.

JIM CRACK CORN (1846)

lyrics and music uncertain

When I was young I us'd to wait
On massa and hand him de plate;
Pass down de bottle when he git dry,
And bresh away de blue tail fly.

Chorus:
Jim crack corn I don't care,
Jim crack corn I don't care,
Jim crack corn I don't care,
Ole massa gone away.

Den arter dinner massa sleep,
He bid dis niggar vigil keep;
An' when he gwine to shut his eye,
He tell me watch de blue tail fly.

Chorus

An' when he ride in de artenoon,
I foller wid a hickory broom;

De poney being berry shy,
When bitten by de blue tail fly.

Chorus

One day he rode aroun' de farm,
De flies so numerous dey did swarm;
One chance to bite 'im on the thigh,
De debble take dat blue tail fly.

Chorus

De poney run, he jump an' pitch,
And tumble massa in de ditch;
He died, an' de jury wonder'd why
De verdic was de blue tail fly.

Chorus

Dey laid 'im under a 'simmon tree,
His epitaph am dar to see:
'Beneath dis stone I'm forced to lie,
All by de means ob de blue tail fly.

Chorus

Ole massa gone, now let 'im rest,
Dey say all tings am for de best;
I nebber forget till de day I die,
Ole massa an' dat blue tail fly.

Chorus

Although the original sheet music names The Virginia Minstrels, a group that helped to originate the blackface minstrel show, as the performers or source of this song, others argue that it was probably composed by Daniel Emmett, the popular songwriter whose "Dixie" is included in this collection.

Simple Gifts (1848)

lyrics and music by Shaker Elder Joseph Brackett, Jr.

'Tis the gift to be simple,
'Tis the gift to be free,
'Tis the gift to come down where we ought
  to be,
And when we find ourselves in the place just
  right,
It will be in the valley of love and delight.

When true simplicity is gained,
To bow and to bend, we will not be ashamed
To turn, turn, will be our delight,
'Till by turning, turning, we come round
  right.

'Tis the gift to be simple,
'Tis the gift to be free,
'Tis the gift to come down where we ought
  to be,

And when we find ourselves in the place just
    right,
Twill be in the valley of love and delight.

This beautiful Shaker hymn has become one of the
most popular of 19th century songs. Composer Aaron
Copland reintroduced the song to 20th century au-
diences.

Susanna (Oh! Susanna) (1848)

lyrics and music by Stephen Collins Foster

I come from Alabama with my Banjo on my
    knee —
I'se gwine to Lou'siana my true lub for to
    see.
It rain'd all night de day I left, de wedder it
    was dry;
The sun so hot I froze to def — Susanna,
    don't you cry.

Chorus:
Oh! Susanna, do not cry for me;
I come from Alabama, wid my Banjo on my
    knee.

I jump'd aboard the telegraph and trabbeled
    down de ribber,
De lectrick fluid magnified, and kill'd five
    hundred Nigga.
De bulgine bust and de hoss ran off, I really
    thought I'd die;

I shut my eyes to hold my bref — Susanna,
   don't you cry.

Chorus

I had a dream de udder night, when ebry
   ting was still;
I thought I saw Susanna dear, a coming
   down de hill.
De buckwheat cake was in her mouf, de tear
   was in her eye,
I says, I'se coming from de souf, — Susanna,
   don't you cry.

Chorus

Perhaps the most important American composer of
the 19th century, Stephen Collins Foster was born
on July 4, 1826 in Lawrenceville, Pennsylvania. As
a teen, Stephen, his brother Morrison, and their close
friend, Charles Shiras, were members of an all-male
secret club, Knights of the S.T., that met twice weekly
in the Foster home, primarily to sing. Some of Foster's
earliest songs were composed for that group, including "Susanna."

At 20, he went to work as a bookkeeper for his brother Dunning's steamship firm in Cincinnati, and there sold some songs and piano pieces to a local music publisher, helping him to launch his career as a composer.

Back in Pittsburgh, he continued to write, working to present the South less nostalgically than others had, and attempting to humanize the characters in his songs, a mission encouraged by his friend Charles Shiras, who was now a local abolitionist leader. Appearances by William Lloyd Garrison and Frederick Douglass further fueled his anti-slavery sentiments, and he collaborated on at least one song with Shiras.

Foster's earliest songs were written as minstrel texts, with many of the stereotypes of the tradition. But his later compositions attempted to humanize Blacks. Nonetheless, his attitude was still a patronizing one, and one of his most noted songs, "Old Black Joe," is seen today as the archetype of the white view of the Black whose societal role remains a subservient one.

DE CAMPTOWN RACES (1850)

lyrics and music by Stephen Collins Foster

De Camptown ladies sing this song,
Doo-da, Doo-da!
De Camptown racetrack's two miles long
Oh, de doo-da day.

Chorus:
G'wine to run all night
G'wine to run all day
I bet my money on a bob-tailed nag
Somebody bet on the gray.

Chorus

I went down South with my hat caved in,
Doo-da, Doo-da!
I came back North with a pocket full of tin.
Oh, de doo-da day.

Chorus

Oh, de long tailed filly and de big black
  horse,
Doo-da, Doo-da!
Come to a mud hole and dey all cut across,
Oh, de doo-da day.

  Chorus

De blind hoss sticken in a big mud hole
Doo-da, Doo-da!
Can't touch bottom wid a ten foot pole,
Oh, de doo-da day.

  Chorus

Old muley cow come on to de track,
Doo-da, Doo-da!
De bob-tail fling her ober his back
Oh, de doo-da day.

  Chorus

Den fly along like a rail-road car,
Doo-da, Doo-da!

Runnin' a race with a shootin' star
Oh, de doo-da day.

Chorus

Seen dem flyin' on a ten mile heat
Doo-da, Doo-da!
Round de racetrack, den repeat
Oh, de doo-da day.

Chorus

I win my money on de bob-tailed nag,
Doo-da, Doo da!
I keep my money in an old tow-bag
Oh, de doo-da day.

Chorus

Written two years after his famed "Susanna," Foster
had recently signed a contract with the New York
music publisher, Firth, Pond, & Co., beginning his
professional career. He had also left his bookkeeping
job in Cincinnati and returned to Pittsburgh early in
the same year.

Old Folks at Home (Swanee River)

(1851)

lyrics and music by Stephen Collins Foster

Way down upon de Swanee ribber,
Far, far away,
Dere's wha my heart is turning ebber,
Dere's wha de old folks stay.
All up down de whole creation,
Sadly I roam,
Still longing for de old plantation,
And for de old folks at home.

   Chorus:
   All de world am sad and dreary,
   Eb'ry where I roam,
   Oh! Darkeys how my heart grows weary,
   Far from de old folks at home.
   [repeated]

All round de little farm I wandered
When I was young,
Dem many happy days I squandered,

Many de songs I sung.
When I was playing wid my brudder
Happy was I.
Oh! Take me to my kind old mudder,
Dere let me live and die.

Chorus

One little hut among de bushes,
One dat I love,
Still sadly to my mem'ry rushes,
No matter where I rove.
When will I see de bees a humming
All round de comb?
When will I hear de banjo tumming
Down in my good old home?

Chorus

"Old Folks at Home" was written during Foster's most productive period in the early 1850s. The work was performed by the Christy Minstrels, but was popular also in the parlor.

WAIT FOR THE WAGON (1851)

*music and lyrics by R. Bishop Buckley
and George P. Knauff*

Will you come with me my Phyllis dear
To yon blue mountain free?
Where the blossoms smell the sweetest,
Come rove along with me.
It's every Sunday morning
When I am by your side,
We'll jump into the wagon
And we'll all take a ride.

    Chorus:
    Wait for the wagon,
    Wait for the wagon,
    Wait for the wagon
    And we'll all take a ride.

Where the river runs like silver
And the birds they sing so sweet
I have a cabin, Phyllis,
And something good to eat;

Come listen to my story,
It will relieve my heart;
So jump into the wagon,
And off we will start.

Chorus

Together, on life's journey,
We'll travel till we stop,
And if we have no trouble,
We'll reach the happy top;
Then come with me, sweet Phyllis,
My dear, my lovely bride,
We'll jump into the wagon,
And all take a ride.

Chorus

A popular campfire song of both Union and Confederate troops, the song is attributed both to R. Bishop Buckley (1810-1867) — the minstrel singer and owner of Buckley's Minstrels — and George P. Knauff. It was first performed in Buckley's Minstrels show.

My Old Kentucky Home, Good Night (1853)

lyrics and music by Stephen Collins Foster

The sun shines bright on my old Kentucky
    home
'Tis summer, the people are gay
The corn top's ripe and the meadow's in
    bloom
While the birds make music all the day
The young folks roll on the little cabin floor
All merry, all happy and bright
By 'n by hard times come a-knocking at the
    door
Then my old Kentucky home, good night.

    Chorus:
    Weep no more my lady,
    Oh weep no more today.
    We will sing one song for the old Kentucky
        home,
    For the old Kentucky home far away.

They hunt no more for the 'possum and the
    coon,
On meadow, the hill and the shore,
They sing no more by the glimmer of the
    moon,
On the bench by that old cabin door.
The day goes by like a shadow o'er the heart,
With sorrow where all was delight.
The time has come when the darkies have to
    part,
Then my old Kentucky home, good night.

Chorus

The head must bow and the back will have
    to bend,
Wherever the darkey may go
A few more days and the trouble will end,
In the field where sugar-canes may grow.
A few more days to tote the weary load,
No matter 'twill never be light,
A few more days till we totter on the road,
Then my old Kentucky home, good night.

Chorus

"My Old Kentucky Home, Good Night" was written at a time in Foster's career in which he was attempting to convince the Christy Minstrels that it was necessary to write more refined texts, without "trashy and really offensive words." He preferred his songs to be performed in a "pathetic" (that is compassionate) manner rather than in a comic style. This song was originally titled "Poor Uncle Tom, Good Night," written in Black dialect to represent the voice of a slave. Foster originally wrote the song in response to Harriet Beecher Stowe's *Uncle Tom's Cabin*.

Hard Times Come Again No More
(1854)

lyrics and music by Stephen Collins Foster

Let us pause in life's pleasures
And count its many tears,
While we sup sorrow with the poor;
There's a song that will linger
Forever in our ears;
Oh hard times come again no more.

Chorus:
Tis the song, the sigh of the weary,
Hard times, hard times,
Come again no more
Many days you have lingered
Around my cabin door;
Oh hard times come again no more.

While we seek mirth and beauty
And music light and gay,
There are frail forms fainting at the door;
Though their voices are silent,

Their pleading looks will say
Oh hard times come again no more.

Chorus

There's a pale drooping maiden
Who toils her life away,
With a worn heart whose better days are
   o'er:
Though her voice would be merry,
'tis sighing all the day,
Oh hard times come again no more.

Chorus

Tis a sigh that is wafted
Across the troubled wave,
Tis a wail that is heard upon the shore
Tis a dirge that is murmured
Around the lowly grave
Oh hard times come again no more.

Chorus

This is one of the few songs by Foster that speaks to the difficulties of everyday life. Most of his lyrics were centered in a nostalgic notion of the past.

Listen to the Mockingbird (1855)

lyrics by Septimus Winner
music by Richard Milburn

I'm dreaming now of Hallie,
Sweet Hallie, sweet Hallie
I'm dreaming now of Hallie,
For the thought of her is one that never dies
She's sleeping in the valley,
The valley, the valley
She's sleeping in the valley,
And the mockingbird singing where she lies.

Chorus:
Listen to the mockingbird,
Listen to the mockingbird,
The mockingbird still singing o'er her grave
Listen to the mockingbird,
Listen to the mockingbird,
Still singing where the weeping willows
    wave.

Ah well I yet remember,
Remember, remember,

Ah well I yet remember,
When we gather'd in the cotton side by side
'Twas in the mild September,
September, September,
'Twas in the mild September,
And the mockingbird was singing far and
  wide.

Chorus

When the charms of spring awaken,
Awaken, awaken
When the charms of spring awaken,
And the mockingbird is singing on the
  bough.
I feel like one forsaken,
Forsaken, forsaken
I feel like one forsaken,
Since my Hallie is no longer with me now.

Chorus

Brother to Joseph Eastburn Winner, author of "The Little Brown Jug," Septimus Winner (1827-1902) was born in Philadelphia. He published numerous songs from the 1850s into the 1880s, including "Abraham's Daughter," "Der Deitcher's Dog" (included in this volume), "Ellie Rhee," "What Care I?" "Whispering Hope," and "Ten Little Indians." He composed under several pseudonyms, including Alice Hawthorne, Percy Guyer, Mark Mason, Apsley Street, and Paul Stenton.

"Listen to the Mockingbird" was one of President Lincoln's favorite songs. It was published by Winner & Shuster in Philadelphia in 1855.

SOME FOLKS (1855)

lyrics and music by Stephen Collins Foster

Some folks like to sigh,
Some folks do, some folks do;
Some folks long to die, —
But that's not me nor you.

> *Chorus:*
> Long live the merry merry heart
> That laughs by night and day,
> Like the Queen of Mirth, —
> No matter what some folks say.

Some folks fear to smile,
Some folks do, some folks do;
Some folks laugh through guile, —
But that's not me nor you.

> *Chorus*

Some folks fret and scold,
Some folks do, some folks do;

They'll soon be dead and cold, —
But that's not me nor you.

Chorus

Some folks get grey hairs,
Some folks do, some folks do;
Brooding o'er their cares, —
But that's not me nor you.

Chorus

Some folks toil and save,
Some folks do, some folks do;
To buy themselves a grave, —
But that's not me nor you.

Chorus

Jingle Bells, or The One Horse Open Sleigh (1857)

lyrics and music by James Pierpont

Dashing thro' the snow, in a one horse open
    sleigh,
O'er the hills we go, laughing all the way;
Bells on bobtail ring, making spirits bright,
Oh what sport to ride and sing a sleighing
    song tonight.

Chorus:
    Jingle bells, jingle bells, jingle all the way;
    Oh! What joy it is to ride in a one horse
        open sleigh.
    Jingle bells, jingle bells, jingle all the way;
    Oh! What joy it is to ride in a one horse
        open sleigh.

A day or two ago, I thought I'd take a ride,
And soon Miss Fannie Bright was seated by
    my side,
The horse was lean and lank; misfortune
    seemed his lot,

He got into a drifted bank, and we, we got
  upsot.

  Chorus

A day or two ago, the story I must tell,
I went out on the snow, and on my back I
  fell;
A gent was riding by, in a one horse open
  sleigh,
He laughed as there I sprawling lie, but
  quickly drove away.

  Chorus

Now the ground is white, go it while you're
  young,
Take the girls tonight, and sing this sleighing
  song;
Just get a bob-tailed bay, two forty as his
  speed,
Hitch him to an open sleigh, and crack,
  you'll take the lead.

  Chorus

James Pierpont (1822-1893) was born, the son of an abolitionist, in Massachusetts. In the 1850s he moved to Savannah, Georgia, where he joined his brother who was minister to a Unitarian congregation. James took a post as the organist and music director, and in 1857, while living in the south, began writing of his New England Christmases in "Jingle Bells." The song, however, was first performed at Thanksgiving, and was so well received that another performance was repeated at Christmas

At the outset of the Civil War, Pierpont joined the Isle of Hope Volunteers to the Confederacy. He survived the war and died in Winter Haven, Florida. His family would again come into national prominence through the work of his nephew, the famed capitalist J. Pierpont Morgan.

The Yellow Rose of Texas (1858)

unknown lyricist and composer

There's a yellow rose in Texas
That I am a going to see
No other darkey knows her
No one only me

> *Chorus:*
> She's the sweetest rose of color
> This darkey ever knew
> Her eyes are bright as diamonds
> They sparkle like the dew
> You may talk about dearest May
> And sing of Rosa Lee
> But the Yellow Rose of Texas
> Beats the belles of Tennessee.

Where the Rio Grande is flowing
And the starry skies are bright,
She walks along the river
In the quiet summer night.
She thinks, if I remember,
When we parted long ago,

I promised to come back again
And not to leave her so.

Chorus

Oh, now I'm going to find her,
For my heart is full of woe,
And we'll sing the song together
That we sang so long ago.
We'll play the banjo gaily,
And we'll sing the songs of yore,
And the Yellow Rose of Texas
Shall be mine forever more.

Chorus

Oh, now I'm headed southward,
For my heart is full of woe.
I'm going back to Georgia
To find my Uncle Joe.
You may talk about your Beauregard
And sing of Bobby Lee,
But the gallant Hood of Texas,
He played hell in Tennessee!

Chorus

Most Americans know this song from the 1955 recording by Mitch Miller, which substantially altered the lyrics. The original lyric appeared around 1836, signed H. B. C., and was dedicated to E. A. Jones (who may or may not have been the individual who was the first African American to graduate from an American university, Amherst College). In any event, the lyric is clearly written by a Black lyricist or one pretending to be. It is believed the song was originally conceived as a folksong recounting the battle of General Sam Houston, who led his brigade of Texas loyalists against the army of General Antonio Lopez de Santa Anna at the Battle of San Jacinto on April 12, 1836.

"Yellow" was a term given to Americans of mixed race, most commonly known as mulattos.

The song was published with music in 1858, and soon became popular worldwide, performed by minstrels both in the US and in Europe. During the civil war, the references to a "darkey" were changed to the word "soldier," and the song became popular as a marching song. The fourth stanza, in fact, was added in 1864 to reflect the hopelessness of General John B. Hood's retreating Texas Brigade after its disastrous Tennessee campaign.

DIXIE (1859)

lyrics and music by Daniel D. Emmett

O, I wish I was in the land of cotton
Old times there are not forgotten
Look away! Look away! Look away! Dixie
Land.
In Dixie Land where I was born in
Early on one frosty mornin'
Look away! Look away! Look away! Dixie
Land.

Chorus:
O, I wish I was in Dixie! Hooray! Hooray!
In Dixie Land I'll take my stand
To live and die in Dixie
Away, away, away down south in Dixie!
Away, away, away down south in Dixie!

Old Missus marry Will, the weaver,
William was a gay deceiver
Look away! Look away! Look away! Dixie
Land.
But when he put his arm around her

He smiled as fierce as a forty pounder
Look away! Look away! Look away! Dixie
  Land.

Chorus

His face was sharp as a butcher's cleaver
But that did not seem to grieve her
Look away! Look away! Look away! Dixie
  Land.
Old Missus acted the foolish part
And died for a man that broke her heart
Look away! Look away! Look away! Dixie
  Land.

Chorus

The most popular song of the South was written by Ohioan Daniel D. Emmet in 1859. A member of "Bryant's Minstrels," then playing in New York, Emmett was asked to provide a new song for the show, and wrote the lyrics and music of "Dixie." The following year, he used the song for a chorus march in New Orleans, and it was immediately taken up by the people and soon became a popular tune for the Confederate Army.

Old Black Joe (1860)

lyrics and music by Stephen Collins Foster

Gone are the days when my heart was young
and gay,
Gone are my friends from the cotton fields
away,
Gone from the earth to a better land I know,
I hear their gentle voices calling "Old Black
Joe."

Chorus:
I'm coming, I'm coming, for my head is
bending low;
I hear their gentle voices calling "Old Black
Joe."

Why do I weep when my heart should feel
no pain
Why do I sigh that my friends come not
again,
Grieving for forms now departed long ago?
I hear their gentle voices calling "Old Black
Joe."

Chorus

Where are the hearts once so happy and so
   free?
The children so dear that I held upon my
   knee,
Gone to the shore where my soul has longed
   to go.
I hear their voices calling "Old Black Joe."

Chorus

Aura Lee (1861)

lyrics by W. W. Fosdick
music by George R. Poulton

When the blackbird in the spring, on the
    willow tree,
Sat and rocked, I heard him sing, singing
    Aura Lee
Aura Lee, Aura Lee, maid of golden hair,
Sunshine came along with thee, and
    swallows in the air.

Chorus:
Aura Lee, Aura Lee, maid of golden hair,
Sunshine came along with thee, and
    swallows in the air.

In thy blush the rose was born, music when
    you spake,
Through thine azure eye the morn, sparkling
    seemed to break.
Aura Lee, Aura Lee, bird of crimson wing,
Never song have sung to me, in the sweet
    spring.

Chorus

Aura Lee! The bird may flee, the willows
    golden hair
Swing through winter fitfully, on the stormy
    air.
Yet if thy blue eyes I see, gloom will soon
    depart,
For to me, sweet Aura Lee is sunshine
    through the heart.

Chorus

When the mistletoe was green, midst the
    winter's snows,
Sunshine in thy face was seen, kissing lips of
    rose.
Aura Lee, Aura Lee, take my golden ring,
Love and light return with thee, and
    swallows with the spring.

William Whiteman Fosdick (1825-1862) was a native of Cincinnati, Ohio. His father was a merchant
and banker, and his mother a noted actress of the

day. Fosdick was known primarily as a poet, the author of *Tecumumseh* and *Ariel and Other Poems* (1855). The composer, George R. Poulton, wrote many standards of the day, including "Rock Me to Sleep Mother" and "Willie Bell."

Some people will recognize the melody of "Aura Lee" to be the same as that Elvis Presley used in his song "Love Me Tender, Love Me True."

THE BATTLE-CRY OF FREEDOM (1861)

lyrics and music by George F. Root

Yes, we'll rally round the flag, boys, we'll
   rally once again,
Shouting the battle-cry of Freedom;
We will rally from the hillside, we'll gather
   from the plain,
Shouting the battle-cry of Freedom.

> *Chorus:*
> The Union forever, hurrah, boys, hurrah!
> Down with the traitor and up with the star;
> While we rally round the flag, boys, rally
>   once again,
> Shouting the battle-cry of Freedom.

We are springing to the call of our brothers
   gone before,
Shouting the battle-cry of Freedom;
And we'll fill the vacant ranks with a million
   free men more,
Shouting the battle-cry of Freedom.

Chorus

We will welcome to our numbers the loyal,
 true and brave,
Shouting the battle-cry of Freedom;
And altho' they may be poor, not a man shall
 be a slave,
Shouting the battle-cry of Freedom.

Chorus

So we're springing to the call from the East
 and from the West,
Shouting the battle-cry of Freedom;
And we'll hurl the rebel crew from the land
 we love the best,
Shouting the battle-cry of Freedom.

Chorus

One of the most popular songs of the Union Army of
the Civil War was composed by George Frederick
Root (1825-1895), one of the most important American composers of the 19th century.

He was a teacher and a publisher who had studied in Europe. The University of Chicago later awarded him a honorary Doctorate degree. Among his many popular songs are "Tramp! Tramp! Tramp!" (included in this volume), "The Vacant Chair," and "Just Before the Battle, Mother" (also included herein).

This song was later used as a campaign song for Lincoln in the 1864 election.

Battle Hymn of the Republic (1862)

lyrics by Julia Ward Howe
music based on "Oh Brothers, Will You Meet Us on Canaan's Happy Shore?" (as adapted by Patrick S. Gilmore's "John Brown's Body")

Mine eyes have seen the glory
Of the coming of the Lord;
He is trampling out the vintage
Where the grapes of wrath are stored;
He hath loosed the fateful lightning
Of His terrible swift sword;
His truth is marching on.

Chorus:
Glory! Glory! Hallelujah!
Glory! Glory! Hallelujah!
Glory! Glory! Hallelujah!
His truth is marching on.

I have seen Him in the watchfires
Of a hundred circling camps
They have builded Him an altar
In the evening dews and damps;

I can read His righteous sentence
By the dim and flaring lamps;
His day is marching on.

Chorus

I have read a fiery gospel writ
In burnished rows of steel:
"As ye deal with My contemners,
So with you My grace shall deal";
Let the Hero born of woman
Crush the serpent with His heel,
Since God is marching on.

Chorus

He has sounded forth the trumpet
That shall never call retreat;
He is sifting out the hearts of men
Before His judgment seat;
Oh, be swift, my soul, to answer Him,
Be jubilant, my feet;
Our God is marching on.

Chorus

In the beauty of the lilies
Christ was born across the sea,
With a glory in His bosom
That transfigures you and me;
As He died to make men holy,
Let us die to make men free;
While God is marching on.

Chorus

Born in New York, Julia Ward Howe (1819-1910) was a daughter of the banker Samuel Ward. In 1843 she married the philanthropist S. G. Howe, head of the Perkins Institute for the Blind. She assisted him in editing his anti-slavery journal, the *Boston Commonwealth*.

In 1861 she made her first trip to Washington, D.C., where she and her husband were invited to a military review in the Virginia camps. On the way back to the city, she heard the song "John Brown's Body" sung to the applause of other soldiers. That evening, with the tune in her head, she wrote the poem which would become almost an anthem to the Northern cause in the Civil War.

Her later life was devoted, in large part, to women's suffrage.

GRAFTED INTO THE ARMY (1862)

lyrics and music by Henry C. Work

Our Jimmy has gone for to live in a tent,
They have grafted him into the Army,
He finally puckered up courage and went,
When they grafted him into the Army.
I told them the child was too young, alas!
At the captain's forequarters, they said he
    would pass,
They'd train him up well in the Infantry
    class,
So they grafted him into the Army.

Chorus:
Oh, Jimmy, farewell!
Your brothers fell
Way down in Alabammy,
I thought they would spare
A lone widder's heir,
But they grafted him into the Army.

Dressed up in his unicorn, dear little chap,
They have grafted him into the Army,
It seems but a day since he sot in my lap,
But they grafted him into the Army.
And these are the trousies he used to wear,
Them very same buttons, the patch and the
    tear,
But Uncle Sam gave him a bran' new pair
When they grafted him into the Army.

Chorus

Now in my provisions I see him revealed,
They have grafted him into the Army,
A picket beside the contented field,
They have grafted him into the Army.
He looks kinder sickish — begins to cry,
A big volunteer standing right in his eye!
Oh, what if the ducky should up and die,
Now they've grafted him into the Army.

Chorus

I've included three other works by the great lyricist-composer Work in this volume: "Grandfather's Clock," "Marching Through Georgia," and "Kingdom Coming."

As the Civil War progressed, it became increasingly necessary to draft men into the armies. The Confederate government ordered, on April 16, 1862, all white males between the ages of 18 and 35 (upped later to the age of 45) to report for three years of service. On March 3, 1863, the Federal government passed the Enrollment Act, which mandated the enlistment of men between 20 and 45.

Both laws allowed the draftee to either send a substitute to serve on his behalf or to pay $300 as an exemption fee. Accordingly, the War quickly was perceived as "a rich man's war and a poor man's fight." There were riots in New York following the first draft lottery, particularly among the Irish. And for four days, they burned and pillaged a Black church and orphanage, the home of the provost marshal, and the offices of the *New York Tribune*. Property damage amounted to over $150,000 before troops were sent to restore order. Work's pun, "grafted," combines the draft with the practice of permitting substitutes or payment.

Beautiful Dreamer (1862)

lyrics and music by Stephen Collins Foster

Beautiful dreamer, wake unto me,
Starlight and dewdrops are waiting for thee;
Sounds of the rude world heard in the day,
Lull'd by the moonlight have all pass'd
   away!
Beautiful dreamer, queen of my song,
List while I woo thee with soft melody;
Gone are the cares of life's busy throng,
Beautiful dreamer, awake unto me!
Beautiful dreamer, awake unto me!

Beautiful dreamer, out on the sea
Mermaids are chanting the wild lorelie;
Over the streamlet vapors are borne,
Waiting to fade at the bright coming morn.
Beautiful dreamer, beam on my heart,
E'en as the morn on the streamlet and sea;
Then will all clouds of sorrow depart,
Beautiful dreamer, awake unto me!
Beautiful dreamer, awake unto me!

Written in 1862, this work was not published until Foster's death in 1864.

JUST BEFORE THE BATTLE, MOTHER (1862)

lyrics and music by George F. Root

Just before the battle, Mother, I am thinking
 most of you
While upon the field we're watching, with
 the enemy in view.
Comrades brave are 'round me lying, filled
 with thoughts of home and God;
For well they know that on the morrow,
 some will sleep beneath the sod.

Chorus:
 Farewell, Mother, you may never press me
 to your breast again;
 But, oh, you'll not forget me, Mother, if I'm
 numbered with the slain.

Oh, I long to see you, Mother, and the
 loving ones at home,
But I'll never leave our banner till in honor I
 can come.
Tell the traitors all around you that their
 cruel words we know,

In every battle kill our soldiers by the help
    they give the foe.

Chorus

Hark! I hear the bugles sounding, 'tis the
    signal for the fight,
Now, may God protect us, Mother, as He
    ever does the right.
Hear "The Battle-Cry of Freedom," how it
    swells upon the air,
Oh, yes, we'll rally 'round the standard, or
    we'll nobly perish there.

Chorus

See "The Battle-Cry of Freedom" for information
about the composer.

KINGDOM COMING (YEAR OF JUBILO)

(1862)

lyrics and music by Henry C. Work

Say, darkies, hab you seen de massa,
Wid de muffstash on his face,
Go long de road some time dis mornin',
Like he gwine to leab de place?
He seen a smoke way up de ribber,
Whar de Linkum gumboats lay;
He took his hat, an lef' berry sudden,
An' I spec' he's run away!

> *Chorus:*
> De massa run, ha, ha!
> De darkey stay, ho, ho!
> It mus' be now de kingdom comin',
> An' de year ob Jubilo!

He six foot one way, two foot tudder,
An' he weigh tree hundred pound,
His coat so big, he couldn't pay de tailor,
An' it won't go half way 'round.

He drill so much dey call him Cap'n,
An' he got so drefful tanned,
I spec' he try an' fool dem Yankees
For to tink he's contraband.

Chorus

De darkeys feel so lonesome libbing
In de loghouse on de lawn,
Dey move dar tings into massa's parlor
For to keep it while he's gone.
Dar's wine an' cider in de kitchen,
An' de darkeys dey'll hab some;
I s'pose dey'll all be cornfiscated
When de Linkum sojers come.

Chorus

De obserseer he make us trouble,
An' he dribe us 'round a spell;
We lock him up in de smokehouse cellar,
Wid de key trown in de well.
De whip is lost, de han'cuff broken,
But de mass'll hab his pay;

He's ole enough, big enough, ought to
  known better
Dan to went an' run away.

Chorus

This song, premiered by the Christy Minstrels, was a huge success, well-received by Blacks and whites of the North. It was said to have been sung by Black soldiers as they marched into Richmond during the conflict's final days. Later the song became popular also in the South.

   See Work's "Grandfather's Clock" for more information on the composer.

Tenting Tonight on the Old Camp Ground (1863)

lyrics and music by Walter C. Kittredge

We're tenting tonight on the old camp
  ground,
Give us a song to cheer
Our weary hearts, a song of home
And friends we love so dear.

  Chorus:
  Many are the hearts that are weary tonight,
  Wishing for the war to cease;
  Many are the hearts looking for the right
  To see the dawn of peace.
  Tenting tonight, tenting tonight,
  Tenting on the old camp ground.

We've been tenting tonight on the old camp
  ground,
Thinking of days gone by,
Of the loved ones at home that gave us the
  hand,
And the tear that said, "Goodbye!"

Chorus

The lone wife kneels and prays with a sigh
That God His watch will keep
O'er the dear one away and the little dears
    nigh,
In the trundle bed fast asleep.

Chorus

We are tenting tonight on the old camp
    ground.
The fires are flickering low.
Still are the sleepers that lie around,
As the sentinels come and go.

Chorus

Alas for those comrades of days gone by
Whose forms are missed tonight.
Alas for the young and true who lie
Where the battle flag braved the fight.

Chorus

No more on march or field of strife
Shall they lie so tired and worn,
Nor rouse again to hope and life
When the sound of drums beat at morn.

Chorus

We are tired of war on the old camp ground,
Many are dead and gone,
Of the brave and true who've left their
    homes,
Others been wounded long.

Chorus

We've been fighting today on the old camp
    ground,
Many are lying near;
Some are dead, and some are dying,
Many are in tears.

Final Chorus:
    Many are the hearts that are weary tonight,
    Wishing for the war to cease;
    Many are the hearts looking for the right,

To see the dawn of peace.
Dying tonight, dying tonight,
Dying on the old camp ground.

Lyricist and composer Walter C. Kittredge was from New Hampshire, and was drafted into the Union Army in the early months of 1863. He had previously been a professional singer, so as he was expected to be sent to the front, he composed this song. In fact, Kittredge was never sent to the front, and did not serve on the battlefield, but was rejected for military service due to medical problems. He later joined the famed Hutchinson Singers and toured with them for 20 years.

All Quiet Along the Potomac (1863)

lyrics by Ethel Beers
music by John Hewitt

All quiet along the Potomac, tonight,
Except here and there a stray picket
Is shot as he walks on his beat to and fro,
By a rifleman hid in the thicket.
'Tis nothing: a private or two now and then
Will not count in the news of the battle;
Not an officer lost — only one of the men,
Moaning out, all alone, the death rattle.
All quiet along the Potomac, tonight.

All quiet along the Potomac, tonight,
Where the soldiers lie peacefully dreaming;
And their tents in the rays of the clear
   autumn moon,
And the light of the camp-fires are gleaming.
A tremulous sigh as the gentle night-wind
Through the forest leaves softly is creeping;
While the stars up above, with their
   glittering eyes,

Keep guard, o'er the army while sleeping.
All quiet along the Potomac, tonight.

There's only the sound of the lone sentry's
    tread,
As he tramps from the rock to the fountain,
And thinks of the two in the low trundle bed
Far away in the cot on the mountain.
His musket falls slack, his face, dark and
    grim,
Grows gentle with memories tender,
As he mutters a prayer for the children
    asleep
And their mother may Heaven defend her!
All quiet along the Potomac, tonight.

The moon seems to shine as brightly as then
That night, when the love yet unspoken,
Leap'd up to his lips, and when low
    murmur'd vows,
Were pledg'd to be ever unbroken
Then drawing his sleeve roughly over his
    eyes,
He dashes off tears that are welling,
And gathers his gun closer up to his breast

As if to keep down the heart swelling.
All quiet along the Potomac, tonight.

He passes the fountain, the blasted pine tree;
And his footstep is lagging and weary;
Yet onward he goes, through the broad belt
   of light,
Towards the shade of the forest, so dreary.
Hark! Was it the night wind that rustles the
   leaves?
Was it the moonlight so wondrously
   flashing?
It looked like a rifle! "Ha! Mary, goodbye!"
And his life blood is ebbing and splashing.
All quiet along the Potomac, tonight.

All quiet along the Potomac, tonight —
No sound save the rush of the river,
While soft falls the dew on the face of the
   dead —
The Picket's off duty forever!

Based on a poem, "The Picket Guard," published in
Harper's Weekly, this song was one of the most popu-

lar during the Civil War. Ethel Lynn Beers (1827-1879) wrote many poems during her lifetime. Composer John Hewitt (1801-1890) was born in Baltimore, Maryland; he composed more than 300 ballads, operas, cantatas, and oratorios. In 1826 he moved to Greenville, South Carolina, but returned to Boston in 1827. In 1840 he became editor of the Washington, D.C. paper *The Capitol*, where he worked for nine years, later securing a position at the Chesapeake Female College in Hampton, Virginia. At the start of the Civil War, he was named drillmaster for the Confederate recruits in Richmond, and later was moved to Savannah. He was the Southern Confederacy's best known composer. Among his songs are "Minstrel's Return from the War," "Hark, Brothers, Hark," "The South Shall Rise Up Free," and "Flag of the Sunny South."

THE ARKANSAS TRAVELER (1863)

lyrics and music generally attributed to
Colonel Sandford C. Faulkner

Oh once upon a time in Arkansas
An old man sat in his little cabin door,
And fiddled at a tune that he liked to hear,
A jolly old tune that he play'd by ear.
It was raining hard but the fiddler didn't
   care
He saw'd away at the popular air,
Tho' his roof tree leaked like a water fall
That didn't seem to bother the man at all.

A traveler was riding by that day,
And stopped to hear him a-practicing away
The cabin was afloat and his feet were wet,
But still the old man didn't seem to fret.
So the stranger said: "Now the way it seems
   to me,
You'd better mend your roof," said he.
But the old man said, as he played away:
"I couldn't mind it now, it's a rainy day."

The traveler replied: "That's all quite true,
But this, I think, is the thing for you to do;
Get busy on a day that is fair and bright,
Then pitch the old roof till it's good and
    tight."
But the old man kept on a-playing at his
    reel,
And tapped the ground with his leathery
    heel:
"Get along," said he, "for you give me a pain;
My cabin never leaks when it doesn't rain."

The Arkansas Traveler was a hit play in the mid 1850s in the taverns of Salem, Ohio. In the play a traveler finds a squatter at a cabin playing this tune, and the entire play revolves around the squatter's efforts to remember the end of the tune, which was played with a great amount of improvisation. The lyrics were credited to David Stevens. However, the words and music are generally now credited to Colonel Sandford C. Faulkner (d. 1875), who traveled across Pope County, Arkansas in the 1840s on a political mission. Faulkner often told the tale of the song at banquets and in barrooms, and he, himself, came to be known as the Arkansas Traveler.

KISSING IN THE DARK (1863)

lyrics by George Cooper
music by Stephen Collins Foster

Sitting in the cosy parlor
When the nights are long,
While the cricket 'neath the window
Sings his dainty song:
With the one we love beside us
And no eyes to mark,
Oh how gaily glide the hours
Kissing in the dark
Oh how gaily glide the hours
Kissing in the dark.

Softly then the vows we murmur
Fall upon the air,
Little hands in ours are folded,
Gently nestling there.
Not a sweeter note of music
Sings the morning lark,
Than is heard when lips are meeting
Kissing in the dark

Than is heard when lips are meeting
Kissing in the dark.

Surely then we grow much bolder
For we know this well,
That we whisper 'neath the shadows
All love bids us tell.
Let us bless the golden hours
With no eyes to mark,
That we pass among the maidens
Kissing in the dark!
That we pass among the maidens
Kissing in the dark!

The lyrics of this song of forbidden love — with the couple evidently forced to kiss in the dark "among the maidens" — might almost be read as a tale of homosexual love and, with its vague reference to "we," could easily be imagined as a statement about its authors. Although I have seen no real evidence that there was a homosexual relationship between the elder Foster and the young lyricist Cooper, it has been suggested on at least one internet website and is hinted at in some of the biographical material. The fact that the great composer had left his wife and family — or that his wife refused to join him in his move to New York — put side by side with the fact that during this period Foster lived a dissolute life of alcoholism, gave rise to a number of unsubstantiated rumors upon his death. Moreover, several of Cooper's lyrics, including, most notably, "Jeff in Petticoats" — in which he writes of Jefferson Davis in woman's apparel, feeling "rather queer" "Just on the out-'skirts' of a wood" — make it clear that Cooper's wit had much in common with what today we would describe as camp or "gay" humor. Finally, in "Dearer Than Life," a song which Foster gave to Cooper as a "memento of friendship" just before Foster's death, Cooper writes lyrics that seem quite inappropriate to a relationship of simple male friendship:

> Tell me you love me again and again!
> Parted from thee, oh? wearisome pain!
> Morn has no beauty to equal thy face,
> Spring has no lilies to equal thy grace!
>
> Dearer to me ever, in joy or in strife,
> Dearer than all art thou, dearer than life!

Given that 19th century same sex friendships were often expressed in a more Romantic sensibility than is currently acceptable, the lyrics here still seem to point to a relationship that was more intimate. All of this is highly speculative. And, of course, the love may have been an unrequited one of a young man for a famed composer.

My Wife Is a Most Knowing Woman

(1863)

lyrics by George Cooper
music by Stephen Collins Foster

My wife is a most knowing woman,
She always is finding me out,
She never will hear explanations
But instantly puts me to rout,
There's no use to try to deceive her,
If out with my friends, night or day,
In a most inconceivable manner,
She tells where I've been right away,
She says that I'm "mean" and "inhuman."
Oh, my wife is a most knowing woman.

She would have been hung up for witchcraft
If she had lived sooner, I know,
There's no hiding anything from her,
She knows what I do — where I go;
And if I come in after midnight
And say "I have been to the lodge,"
Oh, she says while she flies in fury,
"Now don't think to play such a dodge!

It's all very fine, but won't do, man."
Oh, my wife is a most knowing woman.

Now often I go to dinner
And come home a little "so so,"
I try to creep up through the hall-way,
As still as a mouse, on tip-toe,
She's sure to be waiting up for me
And then comes a nice little scene,
"What, you tell me you're sober, you wretch
    you,
Now don't think that I am so green!
My life is quite worn out with you, man."
Oh, my wife is a most knowing woman!

She knows me much better than I do,
Her eyes are like those of a lynx,
Though how she discovers my secrets
Is a riddle would puzzle a sphinx,
On fair days, when we go out walking,
If ladies look at me askance,
In the most harmless way, I assure you,
My wife gives me, oh! such a glance,
And says, "All these insults you'll rue, man."
Oh, my wife is a most knowing woman.

Yes, I must give all of my friends up
If I would like happy and quiet;
One might as well be 'neath a tombstone
As live in confusion and riot.
This life we all know is a short one,
While some tongues are long, heaven knows,
And a miserable life is a husband's
Who numbers his wife with his foes;
I'll stay at home now a true man.
Oh, my wife is a most knowing woman.

This song with its comic lyrics and music-hall wit seems a far cry from Foster's earlier sentimental works. It represents the changes that occurred when he left his family and moved to New York, collaborating with the young poet George Cooper, beginning in 1862. I have included it and another song typical of their collaborations, "There Are Plenty of Fish in the Sea."

There Are Plenty of Fish in the Sea

(1863)

lyrics by George Cooper
music by Stephen Collins Foster

A lady tossed her curls
At all who came to woo;
She laughed to scorn the vows,
From hearts though false or true,
While merrily she sang;
And cared all day for naught.

Chorus:
There are plenty of fish in the sea
As good as ever were caught.
There are plenty of fish in the sea
As good as ever were caught.

Upon their lightning wings
The merry years did glide,
A careless life she led,
And was not yet a bride;
Still as of old she sang
Though few to win her sought.

Chorus

At length the lady grew
Exceedingly alarmed,
For beaux had grown quite shy
Her face no longer charmed.
And now she sadly sings
The lesson time has taught.

Chorus

When Johnny Comes Marching Home (1863)

lyrics and music by Patrick S. Gilmore
(possibly based on the Irish song, "Johnny I Hardly Knew Ye")

When Johnny comes marching home again,
Hurrah! Hurrah!
We'll give him a hearty welcome then
Hurrah! Hurrah!
The men will cheer and the boys will shout
The ladies they will all turn out
And we'll all feel gay,
When Johnny comes marching home.

The old church bell will peal with joy
Hurrah! Hurrah!
To welcome home our darling boy
Hurrah! Hurrah!
The village lads and lassies say
With roses they will strew the way,
And we'll all feel gay
When Johnny comes marching home.

Get ready for the Jubilee,
Hurrah! Hurrah!
We'll give the hero three times three,
Hurrah! Hurrah!
The laurel wreath is ready now
To place upon his loyal brow
And we'll all feel gay
When Johnny comes marching home.

Written by the Union Army bandmaster, Patrick S. Gilmore (1829-1892), "Johnny Comes Marching Home" was one of the most popular songs of the Civil War, and remains popular today. Born in Ireland, Gilmore claimed to have based the song on an Irish folksong, "Johnny I Hardly Knew Ye," but some debate which was written earlier. In Ireland Gilmore was a band member and was introduced to classical and sacred music. In 1848 he immigrated from Ireland to Boston, becoming in a short time the leader of the Boston Brigade Band, and then the Charlestown Band. With the onset of the Civil War, Gilmore, involved with the Salem, Massachusetts band, began playing at recruiting rallies and other military functions. He also composed "John Brown's Body," which later would be rewritten with other lyrics by Julia Ward Howe as "The Battle Hymn of the Republic."

DER DEITCHER'S DOG (1864)

lyrics and music by Septimus Winner

Oh where, Oh where ish mine little dog
  gone,
Oh where, Oh where can he be. . . .
His ears cut short and his tail cut long,
Oh where, Oh where ish he.

> *Chorus:*
> Tra la la la, la la la, la la la, la
> La la la, la la la, la la la, la
> Tra la la, la la la, la

I loves mine lager 'tish very goot beer,
Oh where, Oh where can he be. . . .
But mit no money I can not drink here,
Oh where, Oh where ish he.

Across the ocean in Garmanie,
Oh where, Oh where can he be. . . .
Der Deitcher's dog ish der best companie,
Oh where, Oh where ish he.

Un sasage ish goot, bolonie of course,
Oh where, Oh where can he be. . . .
Dey makes em mit dog und dey makes em
    mit horse,
I guess dey makes em mit he. . . .

Also the composer of "Listen to the Mockingbird,"
Winner was one of the major popular song writers of
19th century America. He was arrested in 1862 for
treason after publishing the song, "Bring Back Pour
Old Commander Little Mac, The People's Pride,"
which sold 80,000 copies before his arrest; he was
released only after destroying the remaining copies.
"Der Deitcher's Dog" was composed from a sense of
humor and caricature of German culture.

SHALL WE GATHER AT THE RIVER?
(BEAUTIFUL RIVER) (1864)

lyrics and music by Robert Lowry

Shall we gather at the river,
Where bright angel feet have trod,
With its crystal tide forever
Flowing by the throne of God?

> *Chorus:*
> Yes, we'll gather at the river,
> The beautiful, the beautiful river;
> Gather with the saints at the river
> That flows by the throne of God.

On the margin of the river,
Washing up its silver spray,
We will talk and worship ever,
All the happy golden day.

> *Chorus*

Ere we reach the shining river,
Lay we every burden down;

Grace our spirits will deliver,
And provide a robe and crown.

Chorus

At the smiling of the river,
Mirror of the Savior's face,
Saints, whom death will never sever,
Lift their songs of saving grace.

Chorus

Soon we'll reach the shining river,
Soon our pilgrimage will cease;
Soon our happy hearts will quiver
With the melody of peace.

Chorus

Robert Lowry has described the experience of writing "Shall We Gather at the River:" "One afternoon in July, 1864, when I was pastor at Hanson Place Baptist Church, Brooklyn, the weather was oppressively hot, and I was lying on a lounge in a state of physical exhaustion. . . . My imagination began to take itself wings. Visions of the future passed before me with startling vividness. The image of the apocalypse took the form of a tableau. Brightest of all were the throne, the heavenly river, and the gathering of the saints . . . and I began to wonder why the hymn writers had said so much about the 'river of death' and so little about the 'pure water of life, clear as crystal, proceeding out of the throne of God and the Lamb.' As I mused, the words began to construct themselves. . . . The music came with the hymn."

Tramp! Tramp! Tramp! (1864)

lyrics and music by George F. Root

In the prison cell I sit,
Thinking Mother dear of you,
And our bright and happy home so far away,
And the tears they fill my eyes
Spite of all that I can do
Though I try to cheer my comrades
    and be gay.

Chorus:
Tramp! tramp! tramp!
The boys are marching
Cheer up comrades,
They will come.
And beneath the starry flag
We shall breathe the air again
Of the free land in our own beloved home.

In the battle front we stood
When their fiercest charge they made,
And they swept us off a hundred men or
    more;

But before we reached their lines
They were beaten back, dismayed,
And we heard the cry of vict'ry o'er and o'er.

Chorus

So within the prison cell
We are waiting for the day
That shall come to open wide the iron door;
And the hollow eye grows bright
And the poor heart almost gay
As we think of seeing home and friends once
 more.

Along with "The Battle-Cry of Freedom," this was
one of Root's most popular songs. The prisoner in
this song is presumably one of the 45,000 Union
soldiers imprisoned at Andersonville prison, formally
known as Camp Sumter. It was the largest of Confederate prisons. Over the course of the Civil War,
almost 13,000 men died in Andersonville from dis-
ease, poor sanitation, malnutrition, overcrowding,
and exposure to the elements.

JEFF IN PETTICOATS (1865)

lyrics by George Cooper
music by Henry Tucker

Jeff Davis was a hero bold,
You've heard of him, I know,
He tried to make himself a king
Where southern breezes blow;
But "Uncle Sam" he laid the youth
Across his mighty knee,
And spanked him well, and that's the end
Of brave old Jeffy D.

   Chorus:
   Oh! Jeffy D.! You "flow'r of chivalree,"
   Oh royal Jeffy D.!
   Your empire's but a tin-clad skirt,
   Oh, charming Jeffy D.

This Davis, he was always full
Of bluster and of brag,
He swore, on all our Northern walls,
He'd plant his Rebel rag;
But when to battle he did go,

He said, "I'm not so green,
To dodge the bullets, I will wear
My tin-clad crinoline."

Chorus

Now when he saw the game was up,
He started for the woods,
His bandbox hung upon his arm
Quite full of fancy goods;
Said Jeff, "They'll never take me now,
I'm sure I'll not be seen.
They'd never think to look for me
Beneath my crinoline."

Chorus

Jeff took with him, the people say,
A mine of golden coin,
Which he, from banks and other places,
Managed to purloin;
But while he ran, like every thief,
He had to drop the spoons.
And maybe that's the reason why
He dropped his pantaloons.

Chorus

Our Union boys were on his track
For many nights and days,
His palpitating heart it beat,
Enough to burst his stays;
Oh! What a dash he must have cut
With form so tall and lean;
Just fancy now the "What is it?"
Dressed up in crinoline!

Chorus

The ditch that Jeff was hunting for,
He found was very near;
He tried to "shift" his base again,
His neck felt rather queer;
Just on the out-"skirts" of a wood
His dainty shape was seen,
His boots stuck out, and now they'll hang
Old Jeff in crinoline.

Chorus

This song, perhaps one of the most hilarious of the Civil War, was based on a true incident. As the Confederacy fell, its President, Jefferson Davis, was forced to flee Richmond, along with his wife and his cabinet. According to Federal cavalrymen who apprehended him on May 10th, he was dressed in his wife's clothing in an attempt to evade capture. Davis claimed to have picked up his wife's raglan by mistake in the dark as he left their tent to investigate the sound of approaching horseman. History has shown that Davis's explanation was probably correct, but the very idea that a Victorian male would dress in female robe, especially to escape capture, would have been seen as highly unmanly. The popular imagination preferred the Tucker-Cooper story.

Marching Through Georgia (1865)

lyrics and music by Henry C. Work

Bring the good ol' Bugle boys! We'll sing
    another song,
Sing it with a spirit that will start the world
    along,
Sing it like we used to sing it fifty thousand
    strong,
While we were marching through Georgia.

Chorus:
    Hurrah! Hurrah! We bring the Jublilee.
    Hurrah! Hurrah! The flag that makes you
      free,
    So we sang the chorus from Atlanta to the
      sea,
    While we were marching through Georgia.

How the darkeys shouted when they heard
    the joyful sound,
How the turkeys gobbled which our
    commissary found,

How the sweet potatoes even started from
   the ground,
While we were marching through Georgia.

Chorus

Yes and there were Union men who wept
   with joyful tears,
When they saw the honored flag they had
   not seen for years;
Hardly could they be restrained from
   breaking forth in cheers,
While we were marching through Georgia.

Chorus

"Sherman's dashing Yankee boys will never
   make the coast!"
So the saucy rebels said and 'twas a
   handsome boast
Had they not forgot, alas! To reckon with
   the Host
While we were marching through Georgia.

Chorus

So we made a thoroughfare for freedom and
   her train,
Sixy miles of latitude, three hundred to the
   main;
Treason fled before us, for resistance was in
   vain
While we were marching through Georgia.

Chorus

Work's famous Civil War song was written shortly
after General Sherman began his march through
Georgia to the sea. But Sherman, himself, grew to
detest the song, having to endure it through numerous performances as he visited various cities of the
nation after the war and traveled to Europe. At one
moment, he pronounced that he would not attend
another encampment until every band in the United
States signed an agreement not to play "Marching
Through Georgia."

See also Work's "Grafted into the Army," "Kingdom Coming," and "Grandfather's Clock" in this
volume.

GOOBER PEAS (1866)

lyrics by A. Pindar
music by P. Nutt

Sitting by the roadside
On a summer's day
Chatting with my mess-mates
Passing time away
Lying in the shadows
Underneath the trees
Goodness how delicious
Eating goober peas.

Chorus:
Peas, peas, peas, peas
Eating goober peas
Goodness how delicious
Eating goober peas.
[Repeated]

When a horseman passes,
The soldiers have a rule
To cry out their loudest,

"Mister, here's your mule!"
But another custom
Enchanting-er than these
Is wearing out your grinders,
Eating goober peas.

Chorus

Just before the battle,
The General hears a row
He says "The Yanks are coming,
I hear their rifles now."
He looks down the roadway
And what d'you think he sees?
The Georgia Militia
Cracking goober peas.

Chorus

I think my song has lasted
Just about enough.
The subject's interesting but
The rhymes are mighty rough.
I wish the war was over

So free from rags and fleas
We'd kiss our wives and sweethearts,
Say goodbye to goober peas.

Chorus

The authors' names of this popular Civil War song
are quite obviously pseudonyms.

The Little Brown Jug (1869)

lyrics and music by Joseph Eastburn Winner

My wife and I lived all alone,
In a little log hut we called our own;
She loved gin and I loved rum,
I tell you what, we'd lots of fun

    Chorus:
    Ha, ha, ha, you and me,
    "Little Brown Jug" don't I love thee;
    Ha, ha, ha, you and me,
    "Little Brown Jug" don't I love thee.

'Tis you who makes my friends my foes,
'Tis you who makes me wear old clothes;
Here you are so near my nose,
So tip her up and down she goes.

    Chorus

When I go toiling to my farm
I take little brown jug under my arm;

Place him under a shady tree;
Little brown jug, 'tis you and me.

Chorus

If all the folks in Adam's race,
Were gathered together in one place;
Then I'd prepare to shed a tear
Before I'd part from you, my dear.

Chorus

If I'd a cow that gave such milk,
I'd clothe her in the finest silk;
I'd feed her on the choicest hay;
And milk her forty times a day.

Chorus

The rose is red, my nose is too;
The violet's blue and so are you;
And yet I guess, before I stop
I'd better take another drop.

Chorus

Joseph E. Winner (1837-1918) was born in Philadelphia, the son of an instrument maker. He and his brother Septimus were partners in the music business and published many musical scores, including his own "Little Brown Jug." Working apart from his brother, Joseph later operated a publishing business. He often composed his compositions under the pseudonym of Eastburn.

SHEW FLY DON'T BOTHER ME (1869)

lyrics by Billy Reeves
music by Frank Campbell

I think I hear the angels sing,
I think I hear the angels sing,
I think I hear the angels sing,
The angels now are on the wing.
I feel, I feel, I feel,
That's what my mother said,
The angels pouring 'lasses down,
Upon this nigger's head.

   Chorus:
   Shew! fly, don't bother me,
   Shew! fly, don't bother me,
   Shew! fly, don't bother me,
   I belong to comp'ny G.
   I feel, I feel, I feel
   I feel like a morning star.
   I feel, I feel, I feel
   I feel like a morning star.

If I sleep in the sun this nigger knows,
If I sleep in the sun this nigger knows,
If I sleep in the sun this nigger knows,
A fly come sting him on the nose.
I feel, I feel, I feel,
That's what my mother said,
Whenever this nigger goes to sleep,
He must cover up his head.

Chorus

This song, described in the original sheet music as a "comic song & dance," was performed by Cool Burgess and Rollin Howard.

Sweet Genevieve (1869)

lyrics by George Cooper
music by Henry Tucker

O, Genevieve I'd give the world
To live again the lovely past!
The rose of youth was dew-impearled;
But now it withers in the blast.
I see thy face in ev'ry dream,
My waking thoughts are full of thee;
Thy glance is in the starry beam
That falls along the summer sea.

Chorus:
O, Genevieve, Sweet Genevieve,
The days may come, the days may go,
But still the hands of mem'ry weave
The blissful dreams of long ago.

Fair Genevieve, my early love,
The years but make thee dearer far!
My heart shall never rove:
Thou art my only guiding star,
For me the past has no regret

What-e're the years may bring to me;
I bless the hour when first we met, —
The hour that gave me love and thee!

Chorus

Composer Henry Tucker (1826-1882) was born in Brooklyn, New York. During 1850 to 1882 he wrote nearly 121 songs and a cantata, "Joseph in Egypt" (1870). Among his most popular songs were "Weep Sad and Lonely," "Jeff in Petticoats," and "A Nation Mourns Her Honored Son."

Lyricist George Cooper was a handsome young man, fifteen years younger than Stephen Foster when he met Foster in New York. In the last years of Foster's life, Cooper collaborated with Foster on over twenty songs, and cared for him after an accident that eventually claimed Foster's life.

REUBEN AND RACHEL (1871)

lyrics by Harry Birch
music by William Gooch

Reuben, Reuben, I've been thinking
What a queer world this would be
If the men were all transported
Far beyond the Northern Sea!

Rachel, Rachel, I've been thinking
What a queer world this would be
If the girls were all transported
Far beyond the Northern Sea!

Chorus:
Too-ral-loo-ral-loo, Too-ral-loo-ral,
Too-ral-loo-ral-loo, Too-ral-lee
[overlapping voices of Reuben and Rachel]
If the men were all transported
Far beyond the Northern Sea.
If we had some more young ladies
On this side the Northern Sea.

Reuben, Reuben, I've been thinking

Life would be so easy then;
What a lovely world this would be
If there were no tiresome men!

Rachel, Rachel, I've been thinking
Life would be so easy then;
What a lovely world this would be
If you'd leave it to the men!

Chorus

Reuben, Reuben, I've been thinking
If we went beyond the seas,
All the men would follow after
Like a swarm of bumble-bees!

Rachel, Rachel, I've been thinking
If we went beyond the seas,
All the girls would follow after
Like a swarm of honey-bees!

Chorus

Silver Threads Among the Gold
(1873)

lyrics by Eben E. Rexford
music by Hart Pease Danks

Darling, I am growing old
Silver threads among the gold
Shine upon my brow today;
Life is fading fast away;
But, my darling, you will be, will be,
Always young and fair to me,
Yes, my darling, you will be,
Always young and fair to me.

Chorus:
Darling, I am growing old,
Silver threads among the gold,
Shine upon my brow today;
Life is fading fast away.

When your hair is silver white,
And your cheeks no longer bright,
With the roses of the May;

I will kiss your lips and say —
Oh! my darling, mine alone, alone,
You have never older grown,
Yes, my darling, mine alone,
You have never older grown.

Chorus

Love can never more grow old,
Locks may lose their brown and gold,
Cheeks may fade and hollow grow,
But the hearts that love will know
Never, never, winter's frost and chill:
Summer warmth is in them still —
Never winter's frost and chill,
Summer warmth is in them still.

Chorus

Love is always young and fair, —
What to us is silver hair,
Faded cheeks or steps grown slow,
To the heart that beats below?
Since I kissed you, mine alone, alone,

You have never older grown —
Since I kissed you, mine alone,
You have never older grown.

Chorus

Composer Hart Pease Danks (1834-1903) was born in New Haven, Connecticut, but grew up in Saratoga Springs, New York, where he studied music with Dr. E. Whiting. Danks worked as a carpenter in his father's construction business before moving into a full career of music. In 1864 he moved to New York City. Among his many hymns and songs are "Not Ashamed of Christ" (1893), "Delphine," "The Lord in Zion Reigneth," and "No Night There." "Silver Threads Among the Gold" sold over three million copies, but Danks had sold the rights and died penniless.

Lyricist Eben E. Rexford (1848-1916) wrote hymns and secular pieces. Born in Johnsburgh, New York, he published his first piece at the age of 14 in the *New York Ledger*.

Bringing in the Sheaves (1874)

lyrics by Knowles Shaw, 1874
melody by George A. Minor, 1880

Sowing in the morning,
Sowing seeds of kindness,
Sowing in the noontide
And the dewy eve;
Waiting for the harvest,
And the time of reaping,
We shall come rejoicing,
Bringing in the sheaves.

Chorus:
Bringing in the sheaves,
Bringing in the sheaves,
We shall come rejoicing,
Bringing in the sheaves.

Bringing in the sheaves,
Bringing in the sheaves,
We shall come rejoicing,
Bringing in the sheaves.

Sowing in the sunshine,
Sowing in the shadows,
Fearing neither clouds
Nor winter's chilling breeze;
By and by the harvest,
And the labor ended,
We shall come rejoicing,
In bringing in the sheaves.

Chorus

Going forth with weeping,
Sowing for the Master,
Though the loss sustained
Our spirit often grieves;
When our weeping's over,
He will bid us welcome,
We shall come rejoicing,
In bringing in the sheaves.

Chorus

Known as "the Singing Evangelist," Knowles Shaw (1834-1878) wrote the lyrics for "Bringing in the

Sheaves," now a traditional thanksgiving hymn, in 1874. Shaw also wrote lyrics for other popular religious songs, including "Give Me That Old Time Religion," "Tarry with Me," and "We Saw Thee Not."

George A. Minor (1845-1904) composed the music in 1880, despite the fact that Shaw had previously composed his own music for his lyrics. But it is Minor's tune that is universally sung today.

GRANDFATHER'S CLOCK (1876)

lyrics and music by Henry C. Work

My grandfather's clock was too large for the
    shelf,
So it stood ninety years on the floor;
It was taller by half than the old man
    himself,
Though it weighted not a pennyweight more.
It was bought on the morn of the day that he
    was born,
And was always his treasure and pride.
But it stopp'd short, never to go again,
When the old man died.

> *Chorus:*
> Ninety years without slumbering
> Tick, tock, tick, tock
> His life seconds numbering,
> Tick, tock, tick, tock
> It stopp'd short, never to go again
> When the old man died.

In watching its pendulum swing to and fro,
Many hours had he spent while a boy;
And in childhood and manhood the clock
   seemed to know,
And to share both his grief and his joy.
For it struck twenty-four when he entered
   the door,
With a blooming and beautiful bride.
But it stopp'd short, never to go again,
When the old man died.

Chorus

My grandfather said, that of those he could
   hire,
Not a servant so faithful he found:
For it wasted no time, and had but one
   desire,
At the close of each week to be wound.
And it kept in its place, not a frown upon its
   face,
And its hands never hung by its side;
But it stopp'd short, never to go again,
When the old man died.

Chorus

It rang an alarm in the dead of the night,
An alarm that for years had been dumb;
And we know that his spirit was pluming its
  flight,
That his hour of departure had come.
Still the clock kept the time, with a soft
  muffled chime,
As we silently stood by his side;
But it stopp'd short, never to go again
When the old man died.

Chorus

Henry Clay Work (1832-1884) was born in Middletown, Connecticut, the son of an abolitionist.

Like his father, Work was also active in the abolitionist movement and was a strong union supporter. His home was a stop on the underground railway, and was instrumental in the escape of thousands of slaves seeking freedom.

In 1853, while working as a printer in Chicago, Work composed his first song, "We Are Coming, Sister May," that became a staple in the repertoire of the Christy Minstrels over the next 10 years. During the Civil War he composed several popular songs, including "Kingdom Coming!" "Grafted Into the Army," "Babylon Is Fallen," "Brave Boys Are They," "Little Major," "God Save the Nation," and "Marching Through Georgia" (later adopted as Princeton University's football song). "Grandfather's Clock" became a successful hit of the 1880s. Others of his songs were included in Minstrel shows and Broadway productions such as *Good Morning Dearie* and *Meet Me In St. Louis*.

Carry Me Back to Old Virginny

(1878)

lyrics and music by James Allen Bland

Carry me back to old Virginny,
There's where the cotton and the corn and
   tatoes grow,
There's where the birds warble sweet in the
   spring-time,
There's where the old darkey's heart am
   long'd to go,
There's where I labored so hard for old
   massa,
Day after day in the field of yellow corn,
No place on earth do I love more sincerely
Than old Virginny, the state where I was
   born.

Chorus:
   Carry me back to old Virginny,
   There's where the cotton and the corn and
      tatoes grow,
   There's where the birds warble sweet in the
      spring-time,

There's where the old darkey's heart am
    long'd to go.

Carry me back to old Virginny,
There let me live 'till I whither and decay,
Long by the old Dismal Swamp have I
    wandered,
There's where the old darkey's life will pass
    away.
Massa and missis have long gone before me,
Soon we will meet on that bright and golden
    shore,
There we'll be happy and free from all
    sorrow,
There's where we'll meet and we'll never
    part no more.

Chorus

James A. Bland (1854-1911) was, perhaps, the greatest Black writer of the American folksong.

    Born in Flushing, New York, one of eight children,
Bland's father was a free man and an alumnus of
Wilberforce University. He received his law degree from

Howard University and was the first Black appointed examiner to the United States Patent Office.

At an early age, living in Philadelphia, the young Bland saw an old black man playing a banjo and singing Black Spirituals, which so excited him that he was determined to have his own banjo. By the age of 14 he had become professional and was entertaining in hotels, restaurants, and private parties. At 15 he began composing his own pieces.

Attending Howard University, Bland met Mannie Friend, for whom he performed one night in Lafayette Park in Washington, D.C. By chance John Ford, owner of the Ford Theater, saw him in the park, which led to Ford's introduction of Bland to George Primrose, one of the great minstrels of the age. In the meantime, Bland composed "Carry Me Back to Old Virginny," which he introduced to Primrose, and which they sang in Baltimore to great success.

Early in his career he performed in D.C. for the Canvas Back Club in Tom Harvey's Restaurant. In attendance were President Cleveland and Robert E. Lee. Over the next few years, the young Bland performed in minstrel shows, eventually joining Colonel Jack Harvey's minstrel troupe, with a salary of $10,000 a year, one of the highest ever paid to a minstrel performer. In a trip to Europe he became an overnight sensation, giving a command performance at Buckingham Palace before Queen Victoria and the Prince of Wales. In 1901, he returned from Europe, penniless. He died of tuberculosis on May 6, 1911.

[See also "Oh, Dem Golden Slippers!" and "In the Evening By the Moonlight."]

Oh, Dem Golden Slippers! (1879)

lyrics and music by James Allen Bland

Oh, my golden slippers am laid away,
Kase I don't 'spect to wear 'em till my
    weddin' day,
And my long-tail'd coat, dat I loved so well,
I will wear up in de chariot in de morn;
And my long, white robe dat I bought last
    June,
I'm gwine to get changed kase it fits too
    soon,
And de ole grey hoss dat I used to drive,
I will hitch him up to de chariot in de morn.

> *Chorus:*
> Oh, dem golden slippers! Oh, dem golden
>   slippers!
> Golden slippers I'm gwine to wear, becase
>   dey look so neat;
> Oh, dem golden slippers! Oh, dem golden
>   slippers!

Golden slippers I'se gwine to wear, To walk
    de golden street.
[repeated]

Oh, my ole banjo hangs on de wall,
Kase it aint been tuned since way las' fall,
But de darks all say we will had a good time,
When we ride up in de chariot in de morn;
Dat's ole Brudder Ben and Sister Luce,
Dey will telegraph de news to Uncle Bacco
    Juice,
What a great camp-meetin' der will be dat
    dey,
When we ride up in de chariot in de morn.

Chorus

So, it's good byc, children, I will have to go
Whar de rain don't fall or de wind don't
    blow,
And yer ulster coats, why, yer will not need,
When yer ride up in de chariot in de morn;
But yer golden slippers must be nice and
    clean,
And yer age must be just sweet sixteen,

And yer white kid gloves yer will have to
   wear,
When yer ride up in de chariot in de morn.

   Chorus

In the Evening by the Moonlight

(1880)

lyrics and music by James Allen Bland

In de ebening by de moonlight when dis
   darkie's work was over,
We would gather round de fire, 'till hoecake
   it was done.
Den we all would eat our supper, after dat
   we'd clear de kitchen,
Dat's only time we had to spare, to hab a
   little fun,
Uncle Gabe would take de fiddle down, dat
   hung upon de wall,
While de silv'ry moon was shining clear and
   bright,
How de old folks would enjoy it, they would
   sit all night and listen,
As we sang in de ebening by de moonlight.

Chorus:
In de ebening by de moonlight, you could
   hear us darkies singing,

In de ebening by de moonlight you could
    hear de banjo ringing.
How the old folks would enjoy it,
They would sit all night and listen,
As we sang in de ebening by de moonlight.

In de ebening by de moonlight when de
    watchdog would be sleeping,
In de corner near de fireplace, beside de ole
    armchair,
What Aunt Chloe used to sit and tell de
    Piccaninnies stories,
And de cabin would be fill'd wid merry
    coons from near and far,
All dem happy times we used to hab, will
    ne'er return again,
Eb'ry thing was den so merry gay and
    bright,
And I nebber will forget it, when our daily
    toll was ober,
How we sang in de ebening by de moonlight.

Chorus

Ring Dem Heavenly Bells (1883)

lyrics and music by Sam Lucas

If you want to get in dem golden gates,
Ring dem heav'nly bells,
Come along, brothers, and don't be late,
Ring dem heav'nly bells,
De gates am gold an' de hinges, too,
Ring dem heav'nly bells,
Dar's plenty of room for me and you,
Ring dem heav'nly bells.

> *Chorus:*
> Gwine to ringer dem heav'nly bells,
> Gwine to ringer dem heav'nly bells,
> Gwine to ringer dem heav'nly bells, good
>   Lord,
> To call dem sinners home.

When de whale was floating down the
    stream,
Ring dem heav'nly bells,
He swallowed up Jonah and didn't he
    scream,

Ring dem heav'nly bells,
Jonah was all dat he had on hand,
Ring dem heav'nly bells,
So he cast him ober on dry land,
Ring dem heav'nly bells.

Chorus

I will tell you now as I've told you before,
Ring dem heav'nly bells,
I'll sing this verse and I'll sing no more,
Ring dem heav'nly bells,
Why, de music lies on Russell's shelf,
Ring dem heav'nly bells,
And if you want any more sing it yourself,
Ring dem heav'nly bells.

Chorus

Sam Lucas (1840-1916), whose real name was Sam
Milady, was one of the most important Black enter-
tainers and composers of the late 19th and early 20th
centuries. He performed with various minstrel
troupes, popularizing many of his own tunes, such

as "Ring Dem Heavenly Bells," "Carve Dat Possum" (one of the so-called "coon" songs), and the non-dialect song, "My Thoughts Are of Thee" (1884) [included in this volume]. The "Russell's shelf" referred to in the last stanza of "Ring Dem Heavenly Bells" is a reference to the publisher of the song, Russell Brothers of Boston.

MY THOUGHTS ARE OF THEE (1884)

lyrics and music by Sam Lucas

Darling I'm lonely, for thee now I sigh;
Give me one glance of thy love beaming eye.
Smile on me now as you smiled long ago.
Lift from my bosom its burden of woe.
Come with thy glances you gave me of yore.
Let me delight in thy presence once more.
Ah! Ah! Love's golden sunshine again let me
    see.

Chorus:
    Near thee or absent my thoughts are of thee.
    Near thee or absent my thoughts are of thee.

Turn not in anger but smile on me now.
Let no dark frown shade thy beautiful brow.
Long have we wandered life's path way
    apart.
Come to me darling, sweet light of my heart.
Thou art my solace when wand'ring afar.
Light of my life and its bright beaming star.

Ah! Ah! Turn not away then my darling
  from me.

Chorus

Bright are the mem'ries of days that are
  gone.
Days when thy heart's fondest love was my
  own.
Sweet were the moments when hope
  beaming high,
Shone on our way like a star in the sky.
Bring back those moments of pleasure again,
Ease my poor heart of its sorrow and pain.
Ah! Ah! Come with thy brightness and
  beauty to me.

Chorus

CLEMENTINE (1885)

lyrics and music by Barker Bradford

In the center of a golden valley,
Dwelt a maiden all divine,
A pretty creature a miner's daughter
And her name was Clementine.

   Chorus:
   Oh my darling, oh my darling,
   My darling Clementine,
   You are lost for me forever,
   Dreadful sorry, Clementine.

Her noble father was the foreman
Of ev'ry valued mine,
And ev'ry miner and ranchman
Was a brother to Clementine.

   Chorus

The foreman miner, an old forty-niner,
In dreams and thoughts sublime,

Lived in comfort with his daughter,
His pretty child Clementine.

Chorus

When far away, he would often pray
That in his sunny clime
No harm might overtake her,
His favorite nugget, Clementine.

Chorus

When the day was done and the setting sun
Its rays they ceased to shine,
Homeward came the brawny miner
To caress his Clementine.

Chorus

None was nearer, none was dearer,
Since the days of forty-nine
When, in youth, he had another
Who was then his Clementine.

Chorus

She led her ducks down to the river,
The weather it was fine,
Stubbed her toe against a sliver,
Fell into the raging brine.

Chorus

He heard her calling: father,
Her voice was like a chime,
But alas he was no swimmer,
So he lost his Clementine.

Chorus

LATER VERSION:

In a cavern, in a canyon,
Excavating for a mine,
Dwelt a miner, forty-niner,
And his daughter Clementine.

Chorus:
Oh my darling, oh my darling,
Oh my darling Clementine,

You are lost and gone forever,
Dreadful sorry, Clementine.

Light she was, and like a fairy,
And her shoes were number nine,
Herring boxes without topses,
Sandals were for Clementine.

Chorus

Walking lightly as a fairy,
Though her shoes were number nine
Sometimes tripping, lightly skipping,
Lovely girl, my Clementine.

Chorus

Drove she ducklings to the water
Ev'ry morning just at nine,
Hit her foot against a splinter,
Fell into the foaming brine.

Chorus

Ruby lips above the water,
Blowing bubbles soft and fine,
But alas, I was no swimmer,
Neither was my Clementine.

Chorus

In a churchyard near the canyon,
Where the myrtle doth entwine,
There grow rosies and some posies,
Fertilized by Clementine.

Chorus

Then, the miner, forty-niner,
Soon began to fret and pine,
Thought he oughter join his daughter,
So he's now with Clementine.

Chorus

I'm so lonely, lost without her,
Wish I'd had a fishing line,
Which I might have cast about here,
Might have saved my Clementine.

Chorus

In my dreams she still doth haunt me,
Robed in garments soaked with brine,
Then she rises from the waters,
And I kiss my Clementine.

Chorus

Listen fellers, heed the warning
Of this tragic tale of mine,
Artificial respiration
Could have saved my Clementine.

Chorus

How I missed her, how I missed her,
How I missed my Clementine,
Til I kissed her little sister,
And forgot my Clementine.

Chorus

JOHNNY GET YOUR GUN (1886)

lyrics and music by Monroe H. Rosenfeld

One evenin' in de month of May,
Johnny get your gun, get your gun,
I met old Peter on de way,
Johnny get your gun, get your gun,
Moses wept and Abram cried,
Johnny get your gun, get your gun,
Satan's coming don't you hide,
Johnny get your gun, get your gun.

Chorus:
Johnny get your gun, get your gun today,
Pigeons a flying all the way,
If you want to get to Heaven in de good ole
    way,
Johnny get your gun, get your gun!

Rolling on,
Rolling on to glory children
Rolling on,
Johnny get your gun, get your gun!

Oh, now good children do yo' best,
Johnny get your gun, get your gun,
And button on your golden vest,
Johnny get your gun, get your gun,
Tell your Uncles and your Aunts,
Johnny get your gun, get your gun,
Fetch along their linen pants,
Johnny get your gun, get your gun.

Chorus

The way am rough wid briar roots,
Johnny get your gun, get your gun,
We'll shoot old Satan 'fore he scoots,
Johnny get your gun, get your gun,
When you hear de rascal yell,
Johnny get your gun, get your gun,
Aim your musket, give him hell,
Johnny get your gun, get your gun.

Chorus

I looked old Satan in the eye,
Johnny get your gun, get your gun,
Said he, I'll want you by an' by,

Johnny get your gun, get your gun,
Fetch me up an Alderman,
Johnny get your gun, get your gun,
Put him in my frying pan,
Johnny get your gun, get your gun.

Chorus

Monroe H. Rosenfeld (1861-1918) was a popular composer, author of numerous successful songs including "I'll Marry the Man I Love" and "By the Dear Old Village Mill Down in the Valley."

There Is a Tavern in the Town (1891)

lyrics and music by F. J. Adams

There is a tavern in the town, in the town,
And there my dear love sits him down, sits
    him down,
And drinks his wine 'mid laughter free,
And never, never thinks of me.

Chorus:
    Fare thee well, for I must leave thee,
    Do not let the parting grieve thee,
    And remember that the best of friends must
        part, must part
    Adieu, adieu, kind friends adieu, adieu,
        adieu,
    I can no longer stay with you, stay with you,
    I'll hang my harp on a weeping willow tree,
    And may the world go well with thee.

He left me for a damsel dark, damsel dark,
Each Friday night they used to spark, used
    to spark,

And now my love once true to me,
Takes that dark damsel on his knee.

Chorus

Oh! Dig my grave both wide and deep, wide
    and deep,
Put tombstones at my head and feet, head
    and feet,
And on my breast carve a turtle dove,
To signify I died of love.

Chorus

Little seems to be known about this composer, and
there is some doubt that Adams was the composer of
this song.

AFTER THE BALL (1892)

lyrics and music by Charles K. Harris

A little maiden climbed an old man's knee,
Begged for a story, "Do Uncle please,"
Why are you single, why live alone?
Have you no babies, have you no home?
I had a sweetheart, years, years, ago,
Where she is now, pet, you will soon know,
List' to the story, I'll tell it all,
I believed her faithless, after the ball.

Chorus:
After the ball is over, after the break of
   morn,
After the dancers' leaving, after the stars are
   gone;
Many a heart is aching, if you could read
   them all;
Many the hopes that have vanished, after
   the ball.

Bright lights were flashing in the Grand
   Ballroom,
Softly the music, playing sweet tunes.
There came my sweetheart, my love my own,
I wish some water, leave me alone!
When I returned dear, there stood a man,
Kissing my sweetheart as lovers can.
Down fell the glass, pet, broken that's all,
Just as my heart was, after the ball.

Chorus

Long years have passed child — I've never
   wed,
True to my lost love, though she is dead,
She tried to tell me, tried to explain,
I would not listen, pleadings were vain,
One day a letter came, from that man,
He was her brother the letter ran,
That's why I'm lonely, no home at all,
I broke her heart, pet, after the ball.

Chorus

With over 300 published songs to his name, in a career that spanned forty years, Charles K. Harris was known as the "king of the tear jerker." Born in Poughkeepsie, New York in 1867, he spent his boyhood in Milwaukee, Wisconsin. Among his many noted songs are "Creep, Baby Creep," "Let's Kiss and Make Up," "Break the News to Mother" (a song about the death of a brave fireman), and "After the Ball." Harris convinced stage performer J. Aldrich Libby to sing it in the popular musical show *A Trip to Chinatown*, whereupon John Philip Sousa heard the tune and played it daily at the Chicago World's Fair, with the result that it became the first musical hit, selling over five million copies.

Daisy Bell (A Bicycle Built for Two) (1892)

lyrics and music by Harry Dacre

There is a flower
Within my heart,
Daisy, Daisy!
Planted one day
By a glancing dart,
Planted by Daisy Bell!
Whether she loves me
Or loves me not,
Sometimes it's hard to tell;
Yet I am longing to share the lot
Of beautiful Daisy Bell!

    Chorus:
    Daisy, Daisy,
    Give me your answer do!
    I'm half crazy,
    All for the love of you!
    It won't be a stylish marriage,
    I can't afford a carriage

But you'll look sweet upon the seat
Of a bicycle built for two.

We will go "tandem"
As man and wife,
Daisy, Daisy!
"Peddling" away
Down the road of life,
I and my Daisy Bell!
When the road's dark
We can both despise
P'licement and "lamps" as well;
There are "bright lights"
In the dazzling eyes
Of beautiful Daisy Bell!

Chorus

I will stand by you
In "wheel" or woe,
Daisy, Daisy!
You'll be the bell(e)
Which I'll ring you know!
Sweet little Daisy Bell!
You'll take the "lead"

In each "trip" we take,
Then if I don't do well,
I will permit you to
Use the brake,
My beautiful Daisy Bell!

Chorus

Although Harry Dacre was British, I've included him in this volume because he wrote the song upon a visit in 1892 to the United States. Upon entering the country, he was forced to pay duty on his bicycle. Complaining to a friend about this, the friend replied, "You're lucky it wasn't a bicycle built for two or you'd have to pay twice the duty!" So was this popular song born.

THE SIDEWALKS OF NEW YORK (1894)

lyrics by Charles B. Lawlor
music by James W. Blake

Down in front of Casey's
Old brown wooden stoop,
On a summer's evening,
We formed a merry group;
Boys and girls together,
We would sing and waltz,
While the "Ginnie" played the organ
On the sidewalks of New York.

   Chorus:
   East side,
   West side,
   All around the town,
   The tots sang "ring a rosie,"
   "London Bridge is falling down;"
   Boys and girls together,
   Me and Mamie Rorke,
   Tripped the light fantastic,
   On the sidewalks of New York.

That's where Johnny Casey,
And little Jimmy Crowe,
With Jakey Krause the baker,
Who always had the dough,
Pretty Nellie Shannon,
With a dude as light as cork,
First picked up the waltz stop
On the sidewalks of New York.

Chorus

Things have changed since those times,
Some are up in "G,"
Others they are wand'rers,
But they all feel just like me,
They would part with all they've got
Could they but once more walk,
With their girl and have a twirl,
On the sidewalks of New York.

Chorus

Lyricist Charles Lawlor (1852-1925) was also a
vaudevillian who performed with James Thornton.

Composer James W. Blake (1862-1935) was a salesman in a hatter's shop. There seems to be some confusion whether Lawlor or Blake wrote the music, but the lyrics were created by both artists.

The Band Played On (1895)

lyrics by John F. Palmer
music by Charles B. Ward

Matt Casey formed a social club that beat
   the town for style,
And hired for a meeting place a hall
When pay day came around each week they
   greased the floor with wax
And danced with noise and vigor at the ball.
Each Saturday you'd see them dressed up in
   Sunday clothes,
Each lad would have his sweetheart by his
   side.
When Casey led the first grand march they
   all would fall in line,
Behind the man who was their joy and pride,
For —

   Chorus:
   Casey would waltz with a strawberry blond,
   And the band played on,
     He'd glide cross the floor with the girl he
     ador'd,

And the band played on,
But his brain was so loaded it nearly
  exploded,
The poor girl would shake with alarm.
He'd ne'er leave the girl with the strawberry
  curls,
And the band played on.
[repeated]

Such kissing in the corner and such
  whisp'ring in the hall,
And telling tales of love behind the stairs
As Casey was the favorite and he that ran
  the ball,
Of kissing and lovemaking did his share.
At twelve o'clock exactly they all would fall
  in line,
Then march down to the dining hall and eat.
But Casey would not join them although
  ev'ry thing was fine,
But he stayed upstairs and exercised his feet,
For —

Chorus

Now when the dance was over and the band
    played home sweet home,
They played a tune at Casey's own request.
He'd thank'd them very kindly for the favors
    they had shown.
Then he'd waltz once with the girl that he
    loved best.
Most all the friends are married that Casey
    used to know,
And Casey too has taken him a wife.
The blond he used to waltz and glide with on
    the ballroom floor,
Is happy missis Casey now for life,
For —

Chorus

This song was first performed by the composer,
Charles Ward, in his vaudeville act in 1895 at Ham-
merstein's Harlem Opera House. It is also one of the
first songs ever promoted by a newspaper, in this case
the *New York World*. It sold over one million copies at
the time of its first publication. This song has been
performed in several movies and in a hit recording in
1941 by Guy Lombardo and his orchestra.

A Hot Time in the Old Town (1896)

lyrics by Joe Hayden
music by Theodore A. Mertz

Come along get you ready wear your bran,
    bran new gown,
For dere's gwine to be a meeting in that
    good, good old town,
Where you know-ded ev'ry body, and dey
    know'ded you,
And you've got a rabits foot to keep away de
    hoodo;
When you hear that the preaching does
    begin,
Bend down low for to drive away your sin
And when you get religion, you want to
    shout and sing,
There'll be a hot time in the old town
    tonight, my baby.

Chorus:
When you hear dem a bells go ding, ling
    ling,
All join 'round

And sweetly you must sing,
And when the verse am through,
In the chorus all join in,
There'll be a hot time in the old town
    tonight.

There'll be girls for ev'ry body in that good,
    good old town,
For dere's Miss Consola Davis and dere's
    Miss Gondolia Brown;
And dere's Miss Johanna Beasely she am
    dressed all in red,
I just hugged her and I kissed her and to me
    that she said;
Please oh please, oh, do not let me fall,
You're all mine and I love you best of all,
And you must be my man,
Or I'll have no man at all,
There'll be a hot time in the old town
    tonight, my baby.

Chorus

Composer Theodore A. Mertz (1848-1936) was born in Hanover, Germany. He was the bandleader for a popular minstrel group, the McIntyre and Heath Minstrels. The first recording of this song, in 1897, was by the ragtime singer Lew Spencer, who helped to make it famous. Teddy Roosevelt's Rough Riders used this song as their "theme song" during the battle of San Juan Hill.

Sweet Rosie O'Grady (1896)

lyrics and music by Maude Nugent

Just down around the corner of the street
  where I reside,
There lives the cutest little girl that I have
  ever spied;
Her name is Rosie O'Grady and, I don't
  mind telling you,
That she's the sweetest Rose the garden ever
  grew.

Chorus:
Sweet Rosie O'Grady,
My dear little Rose
She's my steady lady,
Most ev'ryone knows,
And when we are married,
How happy we'll be;
I love sweet Rosie O'Grady,
And Rosie O'Grady loves me.
[repeated]

I never shall forget the day she promised to
   be mine,
As we sat telling lovetales, in the golden
   summer time,
'Twas on her finger that I placed a small
   engagement ring,
While in the trees, the little birds this song
   they seemed to sing!

Chorus

This song is credited to performer Maude Nugent
(1877-1958), although some have suggested that it
was written by her husband, William Jerome. Publishers refused to publish it and did so only after her
performances made it a hit. It was featured in a 1943
Betty Grable film.

I'll Marry the Man I Love (1897)

lyrics and music by Monroe H. Rosenfeld

One day a rich man called his pretty
  daughter to his side,
And said, "A wealthy friend of mine wants
  you to be his bride;
Last night he spoke to me and I have
  promised him your hand,
So when he calls, say you'll be his —
  remember my command!"
The maiden said, "Why father, dear, I cannot
  be his wife,
Because I love another, yes, far dearer than
  my life!"
And when he sternly told her she must wed
  his choice, instead,
Or else disinherit her, she wept but
  staunchly said:

Chorus:
"I'll marry the man I love . . .
No other my hand shall claim . . .
For I've given my heart to him, dad,

And someday I'll bear his name.
Remember that gold can't buy
Or conquer a woman's heart.
And I'll marry the man I love, dad,
Tho' from you I part!"

In anger proud he stormed and raged, then
   pointing to the door,
Said: "Go! I cast you off, and let me see your
   face no more!
You've dared to disobey me but your folly
   you'll repent!
For out of all my millions you shall never
   have a cent!"
She sadly turned to go but stopped beside
   the door to say:
"'Tis you, I fear, who will regret your cruel
   words this day!"
And when he said, "Well, I'll forgive if you
   will only wed
The man I've chosen for you dear," once
   more she bravely said:

Chorus

GREEN INTEGER
Pataphysics and Pedantry

Douglas Messerli, *Publisher*

Essays, Manifestos, Statements, Speeches, Maxims,
Epistles, Diaristic Notes, Narratives, Natural Histories,
Poems, Plays, Performances, Ramblings, Revelations
and all such ephemera as may appear necessary
to bring society into a slight tremolo of confusion
and fright at least.

*

RECENT GREEN INTEGER TITLES

100 Gertrude Stein *Three Lives* $12.95
106 Louis-Ferdinand Céline *The Church* $13.95
107 John O'Keefe *The Deatherians* $10.95
108 Francis Carco *Streetcorners* $12.95
109 Thomas Mann *Six Early Stories* $10.95
116 Oswald Egger *Room of Rumor: Tunings* $9.95
117 Deborah Meadows *Representing Absence* $9.95
119 Reina María Rodríguez *Violet Island and Other Poems* $12.95
126 Ingeborg Bachmann *Letters to Felician* $9.95
147 Douglas Messerli *First Words* $10.95